Socrates' Children
The 100 Greatest Philosophers
Volume II: Medieval Philosophers

# Socrates' Children
# The 100 Greatest Philosophers
## Volume II: Medieval Philosophers

Peter Kreeft

ST. AUGUSTINE'S PRESS
South Bend, Indiana

Manufactured in the United States of America.

1  2  3  4  5  6    25  24  23  22  21  20  19

**Library of Congress Cataloging in Publication Data**
Names: Kreeft, Peter, author
Title: Socrates' children. Medieval / Peter Kreeft.
pages cm. — (The 100 greatest philosophers; volume II)
Includes bibliographical references and index.
ISBN 978-1-58731-784-2 (paperback: alk. paper)
1. Philosophy, Medieval. 2. Philosophers, Medieval. I. Title.
B721.K74 2015
189—dc23        2015005663

∞  The paper used in this publication meets the minimum requirements of the American National Standard for Information Sciences - Permanence of Paper for Printed Materials, ANSI Z39.48-1984.

St. Augustine's Press
www.staugustine.net

to William Harry Jellema,
Brand Blanshard,
Balduin Schwarz,
and W. Norris Clarke, S.J.

who taught me how to philosophize

# Contents

\* indicates important philosophers
\*\* indicates very important philosophers

# A Salesman's-Pitch Introduction to This Book

## Why the History of Philosophy Is the Best Introduction to Philosophy

There are two ways to teach and learn philosophy: the usual way and the best way. The usual way is called "analytic philosophy." This means arguing about the questions philosophers ask, using modern symbolic logic. There's certainly nothing wrong with that, but it does not appeal to most people. It's abstract. Ordinary people, as distinct from philosophers, don't really care about a technical logical proof that there is a self-referential inconsistency in the hypothesis that consciousness is an epiphenomenon of matter, or a ten-step proof that there is in principle no possible proof that you really have a body. (Yes, those are the kind of questions "analytic philosophers" actually write about.

There have been two very different conceptions of philosophy in the English speaking world for the last century. Traditionally, philosophy was about life, and it was something to be lived. Philosophers were looked up to as "wise men" rather than "wise guys." Philosophical reason was something computers simply did not have. But ever since (1) Russell and Whitehead's *Principia Mathematica*, in 1910, 1912, and 1913, (2) Wittgenstein's *Tractatus,* in 1921, and (3) Ayer's *Language, Truth and Logic,* in 1936, there has been a new conception of the task of the philosopher: (a) not to tell us what is, but to analyze the language of those who do; and (b) in so doing to imitate scientific and mathematical thinking, which is "digital," rather than ordinary language, which is "analog"; and, to that end, to use symbolic, or mathematical, logic (basically, computer logic) rather than traditional Aristotelian ordinary-language logic.

Indeed, this has been the "main line" conception of philosophy in English-speaking cultures for over half a century. It has moved far beyond the early, narrow, and dogmatic claims for it, such as Ayer's, but its *style* of philosophical writing is still easily identifiable: you can spot an "analytic philosopher" by reading just one paragraph.

Such philosophers are useful as vacuum cleaners and garbage collectors are useful, to identify and dispose of waste. They clean well. But they do not cook very tasty or interesting meals. I think large philosophy departments should have at least one and at most two of them, as restaurants should have cleaning crews.

The best way to teach philosophy is by a story: the dramatic story of the history of philosophy, the narrative of "the great conversation" which you find in "the great books." It's politically incorrect to say it, but there is indeed a canon or list of "great books." That's why Plato and Shakespeare never die. Of course the canon is arguable and not sacrosanct. It's only human. It's not a canon of sacred scriptures.

1

The most effective way to teach *anything* is by a story, a narrative. All the great teachers used stories, parables, examples, analogies, illustrations. It's really very easy to get ordinary human beings interested in philosophy: just put the picture back into the frame; put the abstract, difficult questions that philosophers ask back into the context of history, where they actually came from: the real, lived human conversations and arguments that passionately divided real individuals, like Socrates and the Sophists, and whole cultures like ancient Rome and medieval Christendom and modern secular scientific democracies.

The primary reason why the history of philosophy works better than analytic philosophy, the primary reason why most students love it and often become philosophers and philosophy teachers through it, is embarrassingly simple: because the great masters of the past are more *interesting* than present day philosophers.

If we are too arrogant to admit that, we judge the past by the standards of the present; the opposite idea hardly ever even occurs to us. So we study the past not to learn from them but to teach them, to show how primitive they were compared to ourselves. I refute this "chronological snobbery" by three simple words: Socrates, Plato, Aristotle.

The sciences progress almost automatically; the humanities do not. Philosophy is one of the humanities, not one of the sciences.

Our ancestors made mistakes, just as we do, but different ones. Theirs are now usually obvious to us; our own are not, and therefore are much more harmful. They are the glasses through which we look rather than the things we look at. "To see ourselves as others see us" is to broaden our mind. We wonder how we will we appear to our remote descendants, but we cannot know. We cannot read the books that haven't been written yet. But we can know how we would look to our remote ancestors. For we can read their books.

The only alternative to listening to the many who have already spoken, and died, is listening to the few who are now alive and speaking: ourselves. The first, often called "tradition," is more democratic. It is what Chesterton called "the democracy of the dead": extending the vote to those who otherwise would be disqualified not by accident of birth but by accident of death.

A scientist studies the history of science as a series of instructive errors and gradual progress to enlightenment. And this is right, in science, because in science the past really is inferior to the present, and has been proved to be that. But it is not right to do this in philosophy because philosophy is not science, and past philosophers have *not* been proved to be inferior to present ones. Here is a proof of that fact—or, rather, of the fact that at least unconsciously *we believe that* they were wiser than we are, and not vice versa: We do not speak of "modern wisdom" but of "ancient wisdom." The noun we spontaneously connect with "modern" is not "wisdom" but "knowledge." Knowledge is incremental, like a stairway: it naturally progresses. Wisdom is not. And philosophy is the search for wisdom.

The best way to learn philosophy, then, is through its history. This is true even if your eventual goal is to be an "analytic philosopher" and analyze the issues logically and not historically (which is a perfectly legitimate and necessary job). For you simply can't find any better teachers to begin with than the ancients, especially Socrates, Plato, and Aristotle, even if you want to move beyond them.

The history of philosophy is not dead facts but living examples. It is not to be studied simply for its own sake. We should apprentice ourselves to the great minds of the past for our sakes, not for theirs; for the sake of the present and the future, not the past.

I have tried just about every possible way to introduce philosophy to beginners (and some impossible ways too), and by far the most effective one I have ever found is the "great books," beginning with the dialogs of Plato.

If Plato was the first great philosophical *writer*, Socrates, his teacher, was the first great *philosopher*. Plato was to Socrates what Matthew, Mark, Luke, John, and Paul were to Jesus. (Socrates, like Jesus and Buddha, wrote nothing. He was too busy *doing* it to publish it.) And Aristotle, Plato's prime pupil, is to the West what Confucius is to China: the archetype of common sense, the one whom subsequent thinkers either build on as a primary foundation or attack as a primary opponent.

So here is the story of philosophy. It's the story of a long, long series of arguments in a very large and dysfunctional family, and Socrates is its main patriarch, so I've called it "Socrates' Children."

## Something about Passion

Most philosophy textbooks aren't fully human because they deliberately cut out all emotions, such as enthusiasm and wonder—even though Socrates, Plato, and Aristotle all said that wonder was the origin of philosophy! Most textbook authors try to imitate computers. I gladly announce that I am not a computer. I am a person, with both rational and irrational passions, and feelings. One of these is the passion for philosophy, and the conviction that philosophy should be exciting—rather, that it *is* exciting, and therefore should be taught that way. I am convinced that reason and passion, head and heart, are both very, very valuable and ought to be allies, not enemies.

The purpose of an introduction to philosophy is to intro-duce philo-sophy, that is, to lead-into (the literal meaning of "introduction") the-love-of-wisdom (the literal meaning of "philosophy"). To-lead-*into*, not merely to-see-and-analyze-from-afar. To be a door, not a microscope. And to lead the reader into the-love-of-wisdom, not the-cultivation-of-cleverness.

Love is a passion. Without blood from the heart, the brain does not work well. Without the will to understand, we do not understand. The brain is not merely a computer; it is a *human* brain. My ambition in this book is not just to inform and to summarize historical facts. I want to be your matchmaker. Jack and Jill, come up the hill and meet Plato. Fall in love with him. Struggle, be puzzled, get angry, fight your way out of the Cave. This book is not just *data,* this is drama.

## Why This Book?

I decided to write this book when the umpteenth person asked me the following question: "Could you recommend just one book that covers the whole history of philosophy that beginners can understand and even get excited about?"

Since I could not answer that question in words, I decided to try to answer it in deeds. I write the books I want to read when nobody else will write them. Sometimes you have to write a book first in order to get the satisfaction of reading it.

Thirty two features make this book distinctive.

(1) **It is "existential," practical, personal**. Philosophy is about *human* life and thought, so I concentrated on the ideas that *make a difference* to our experience, to our lives. That is William James' "pragmatic criterion of truth." (I think he really meant 'meaning' rather than 'truth.') His point is that if you can't specify *what difference it makes* if you believe or disbelieve an idea, then that idea is neither true nor false in any humanly significant sense.

(2) **It is selective.** It doesn't try to cover too much. For an "introduction" means, literally, a "leading-into" rather than a summary or survey. It is not the last word but a first word, a beginning; for it is for beginners. Little philosophers get only a page or two, great philosophers get only a dozen, medium sized philosophers get between 3 and 6.

(3) **It concentrates on "the Big Ideas."** (In fact, I thought of entitling it "What's the Big Idea?") This involves minimizing or omitting many "smaller" ideas. I think it is true of ideas, as of friends, that you can have too many of them. Better to have a few that are deeply understood and cherished than to have many that are not.

This book includes only what most students will find valuable. They will find valuable only what they remember years later. They will remember years later only those ideas that make a difference to their lives. And that's usually one Big Idea from each philosopher.

(4) **It covers 100 philosophers.** I chose them by two standards: (a) intrinsic excellence, wisdom, and importance, and (b) extrinsic historical influence and fame.

(5) **It gives much more space to the 'big nine': Socrates, Plato, Aristotle, Augustine, Aquinas, Descartes, Hume, Kant, and Hegel.** These are the most influential philosophers of all time.

(6) **It presents the history of philosophy as a story, a "great conversation."** A book about the history of philosophy is not about history but about philosophy; yet philosophers can be understood best historically: as partners in a dialog with other philosophers. The

whole history of Western philosophy is a very long and complex Socratic dialog. The dialog is exciting, for thought-revolutions are more important than political revolutions, and battles between ideas are more intriguing than battles between armies.

(7) On the other hand, **its point of view is not historical relativism.** I do not try to explain away any philosophers by reducing them to creatures of their times, as Marxists and Hegelians do. Though humans are rooted in *humus (*earth) like trees, yet like trees we also reach into the sky. Historians read the *Times* but philosophers try to read the eternities.

(8) **It is for beginners, not scholars.** It is not "scholarly" in style. It does not break new ground in content. It does not push any new philosophical theory.

(9) **It is not "dumbed down"** even though it is for beginners, for it is for intelligent beginners, not dumb beginners. (It is also appropriate for intelligent high school seniors and for graduate students in other departments than philosophy.)

(10) **It is for college courses** in the history of philosophy. **But it is also a "do-it-yourself" book** which does not require a teacher to interpret it.

(11) **Its point of view is traditional rather than fashionable.** It neither assumes nor tries to prove any one particular philosophical position. Though I try to be fair to all philosophers and get "into their heads" of each, I confess at the outset **a sympathy for common sense**. In philosophical terms, this usually (but not always) means, in one word, Aristotle rather than, e.g., Nietzsche, Marx, or Derrida.

(12) **It tries to be both clear and profound, both logical and existential.** For two or three generations philosophers have been divided into two camps separated by these two ideals. English speaking "analytic" philosophers have sought maximum clarity and logic, while Continental philosophers have sought a more "synthetic" "big picture" that is more profound and existential. The result is that the former sound like chirping birds while the latter sound like muttering witch doctors. I try to bridge this gap by going back to Socrates, who demanded both clarity and profundity. Many other philosophers today are also trying to bridge that gap by dialoging with each other across the Channel.

(13) Like Socrates, it takes logic seriously. Therefore **it summarizes not just conclusions but arguments**, and evaluates them logically. But it uses ordinary-language logic, common-sense logic, Socratic logic, rather than the artificial language of modern mathematical, symbolic logic.

(14) **It uses three kinds of logic**, as Socrates did:

5

It uses *inductive* logic by grounding and testing its abstract and general ideas in concrete and particular instances.

It uses *deductive* logic in tracing practices back to their principles and principles back to their premises, and in following premises, principles, and practices out to their logical conclusions.

And it uses *seductive* logic as a woman would seduce a man by her beauty. For philosophy can be very beautiful.

(15) Many of the questions philosophers ask are also questions religion claims to answer, though the methods of these two enterprises are fundamentally different: philosophy uses human reason alone while religion relies on faith in something that is more than human. Therefore this book **naturally interfaces with religion** in its questions, but not in its methods. Neither religious belief nor unbelief is either presupposed or aimed at.

(16) **It is so unfashionable as to seek *truth*, of all things!** Much of contemporary philosophy looks like intellectual masturbation. But real philosophy ("the love of wisdom") seeks the fruit of truth, not just fun, play, or display of cleverness. It is not mentally contraceptive.

(17) **It emphasizes the classical philosophers,** for two reasons.

(1) We don't yet know which contemporary philosophers will be acknowledged as great and which will be forgotten. It takes time for history, like a sieve, to sort out the big and little stones. Every era makes mistakes about itself. "Our era is the only one that doesn't" is perhaps the stupidest mistake of all.

(2) The questions contemporary philosophers typically ask are not the questions real people ask. They are questions like whether we can prove that we're not just brains in vats being hypnotized into seeing a world that isn't there. How many people do you know who worry about that question? I suspect even philosophers don't really worry about it if they're sane; they just pretend to. (In other words, they pretend to be insane.) Real people ask questions like: What are we? What should we be? Why were we born? Why must we suffer? Why must we die? Why do we kill? How should we live? Is there a God? An afterlife? Where does morality come from? What is the greatest good? How do you know?

(18) **It is full of surprises.** It emphasizes things readers probably do *not* already know, understand, or believe. It does not patronizingly pass off clichés as profundities. It emphasizes wonder, since "philosophy begins in wonder."

This does not contradict its preference for common sense (point 7 above), for common sense, when explored, turns out to be more wonderful than any cleverly invented ideologies. For real life is much more fantastic than any fantasy; for fantasy only imitates life, while life imitates nothing. (You can learn this, and similar things, from the most maverick pick among my 100 philosophers, G.K. Chesterton.)

(19) **It dares to be funny.** It includes humor whenever relevant, because reality does. Reality is in fact amazingly funny.

(20) **It includes visual aids** because we both learn and remember more effectively with our eyes than with our ears.

The treatment of each of the 100 philosophers usually contains **12 parts**, as follows:

(21) A photo, statue, or **portrait** of the philosopher

(22) A brief **bio**, including **the seven W's**:
   (a) **"Who"**: his complete name
   (b) **"Where"**: his place of birth and nationality
   (c) **"When"**: his birth and death
   (d) **"What"**: his job or career
   (e) **"Whimsy"**: unusual, dramatic or humorous facts or legends about him
   (f) **"Which"** was his most famous book
   (g) **"Why"** he asked the questions he did, which is point (23) below:

Obviously, some philosophers' lives are much more interesting than others. Some philosophers are almost all life and hardly any theory (e.g. Diogenes the Cynic); others are almost all theory and almost no life (e.g. Hegel).

(23) His **historical situation** and problem, his dialog with previous philosophers

(24) His **Big Idea** or central insight or most important teaching

(25) His most **famous quotation(s)** (You will find the following piece of advice unusual but practical, I think. When you come to a quotation from a philosopher in this book, long or short, read it *aloud*. This helps you to remember and also to more deeply understand it, because this not only reinforces one sense [seeing] with another [hearing] but also brings into play your unconscious mind, your intuition and feelings.)

(26) A **diagram** or sketch whenever possible, translating the abstract idea into a visual image

(27) The **practical difference** the idea makes
   (a) to life—to *your* life;
   (b) to thought (the idea's logical implications); and
   (c) to history (to subsequent thinkers)

(28) The essential **argument(s) for** this idea

(29) The essential **argument(s) against** it

(30) **Satellite ideas**, if any

(31) Short recommended **bibliography**, both primary and secondary sources, but only when readable and helpful

(32) **Probable reading experience;** hints to make him come clear and alive.

# A Very Short Introduction to Philosophy

The best introduction to philosophy is the history of philosophy. The best answer to the question "What is philosophy?" is not an ideal definition of it but real examples of it. If you want to know what philosophy is, read philosophers.

Start with Plato. Whitehead famously summarized the whole history of Western philosophy as "**footnotes to Plato**." (I thought of using that for the title of this book.). Plato is the first philosopher from whom we have whole books. He is the first great philosophical writer, *and the last.* For no philosopher has ever improved on his style.

Philosophy, according to its three greatest inventors, Socrates, Plato, and Aristotle, begins in wonder and ends in wisdom. It is, literally "the love (*philia,* friendship) of wisdom (*sophia).*"

"Wonder" means three things:

(a) It starts with *surprise* (e.g. "What a wonder!—that despite my deepest desire to live, I must die!"),

(b) It leads to *questioning* (e.g. "I wonder *why* I must die."),

(c) It ends with deepened *appreciation* (e.g. "How wonderful that my life, like a picture, has a frame, a limit! How wonderful that what I so deeply fear—death—I also deeply need!").

The first kind of wonder (surprise) leads to the second (questioning). We question only what we find remarkable. And the second kind of wonder (questioning), when successful, leads to the third kind (appreciation, contemplative wonder): we contemplate, and appreciate, and intellectually "eat," the truths we discover through questioning and investigating and reasoning.

What do philosophers ask questions about? These are the *divisions* of philosophy. They include 4 main parts:

(1) *metaphysics*, which is the study of the truths, laws, or principles that apply to all reality, not just physics but "beyond" (*meta)* those limits, though including them

(2) *philosophical anthropology*, or philosophical psychology, which is the philosophical study of human nature, or the self

(3) *epistemology*, which is the study of knowing and how we know; this can include logic and methodology

(4) *ethics*, which is the study of what we ought to do and be

In other words,

(1) What is real?

(2) What am I?

(3) How can I know?

(4) What should I do?

But philosophers also apply philosophy to many other areas, such as

(5) social and political philosophy

(6) philosophy of religion

(7) philosophy of education

(8) philosophy of art, or aesthetics

(9) philosophy of science

Etc. We can philosophize about anything: sexuality, sports, humor, even soup. E.g. I wrote a philosophy of surfing entitled *I Surf, Therefore I Am*

Why is philosophy important?

(1) Because it is distinctively human. Animals do not philosophize because they know too little, and God, gods, or angels do not philosophize because they know too much. To be human is to philosophize, for to be human is to wonder.

(2) Because it makes a difference to everything. Sometimes the difference is a matter of life or death. Wars are fought for philosophical reasons. The Civil War was fought over the rightness or wrongness of slavery. World War II was fought over Fascism, which was a philosophy. The Cold War was fought over a philosophy: Marxism, or Communism. The present "culture wars" are being fought throughout Western civilization over many related philosophical issues: religion, human nature, "natural laws," human sexuality, the meaning of marriage and family, whether human lives have absolute or relative value, just and unjust wars, and the role of the State in human life.

For a short but dramatic introduction to philosophy, I recommend you read four of the dialogs of Plato that center around the death of Socrates, the first great philosopher: *Euthyphro, Crito," Apology*, and *Phaedo*. Or—a very distant second best—read my *Philosophy 101 by Socrates: An Introduction to Philosophy via the "Apology" of Plato*.

The best way to learn philosophy is not through books *about* the philosophers—books like this one—but from the books written *by* the philosophers. Fortunately, most great philosophers wrote short, simpler books as well as long, harder ones; and almost always it was the shorter ones that became classics. For instance;

| Philosopher | easy, short book | hard, long book |
|---|---|---|
| Plato | *Apology* | *Republic* |
| Augustine | *Confessions* | *City of God* |
| Boethius | *The Consolation of Philosophy* | *On the Trinity* |
| Anselm | *Proslogium* | *Monologium* |
| Bonaventure | *Itinerary of the Mind to God* | *many* |
| Machiavelli | *The Prince* | *Discourses* |
| Pascal | *Pensées* | *Provincial Letters* |

| | | |
|---|---|---|
| Descartes | *Discourse on Method* | *Meditations* |
| Leibnitz | *Monadology* | (many) |
| Berkeley | *Three Dialogs Hylas & Philonous* | (many) |
| Hume | *Enquiry on Human Understanding* | *Treatise on Human Nature* |
| Kant | *Grounding of Metaphysic of Morals* | *Critique of Practical Reason* |
| Heidegger | *Discourse on Thinking* | *Being and Time* |
| Sartre | *Existentialism & Human Emotions* | *Being & Nothingness* |
| Marx | *Communist Manifesto* | *Capital* |
| Kierkegaard | *Philosophical Fragments* | *Concluding Unscientific Postscript* |
| Marcel | *The Philosophy of Existentialism* | *The Mystery of Being* |

Unfortunately, four of the most important philosophers—Aristotle, Aquinas, Hegel, and Nietzsche—never wrote a short, clear and simple book (though Aristotle wrote a long and simple one, the *Nicomachean Ethics,* Nietzsche wrote a few short but not simple ones, and Aquinas wrote a very long and clear but not simple one, the *Summa Theologiae).*

## Philosophy and Religion

Philosophy is not religion and religion is not philosophy.

All religions, however diverse their content, originate in faith rather than pure reason, and their ultimate appeal is to divine authority, the authority of divinely revealed scriptures (e.g. Bible, Qur'an), or institutions (e.g. the Catholic Church), or mystical experiences (e.g. Buddhist "Nirvana").

Philosophy, classically conceived, originates in and is justified by appeal to reason. Medieval philosophers often used philosophical reason to justify religious faith (e.g. rational proofs for the existence of God). Ironically, modern philosophers, in reaction against medieval philosophy, often begin by questioning the validity of faith and end by questioning the validity of reason and substituting ideology, feeling, or will (e.g. Hobbes, Hume, Rousseau, Kant, Fichte, Schopenhauer, Nietzsche, Dewey, Derrida). Philosophers who make this move usually construe "reason" much more narrowly than classical (premodern) philosophers did. They think of "reason" as *scientific* reasoning. If medieval philosophy is in bed with religion, modern philosophy is in bed with science.

The greatest difference between philosophers and other human beings is probably not philosophy but religion. For everyone has a philosophy, whether well thought out or not, but not everyone believes in a religion. According to the polls, only 5–10% of Americans identify themselves as atheists, but 75% of philosophers do. That fact explains why most histories of philosophy do not understand religious philosophies very well. Religion, like sex, humor, and music, is something one understands from within much better than from without. Whenever I have my class argue about religion, I make the believers argue for atheism and the doubters, agnostics, and atheists argue for faith, and the result is always the same: the pretend atheists do a far better job than the pretend believers. Then we argue about whether this was because only the believers understood both sides or whether it was because the pretend believers had to argue for unarguable myths and superstitions.

This book is not about religion but about philosophy, but one of the primary questions of philosophy is whether something like God exists; for this idea makes more of a difference to everything else, both in life and in philosophy, than just about any other idea. It makes a difference to personal identity, death, morality, and "the meaning of life." The God-idea is almost certainly either the most important error and illusion or the most important truth in the history of human thought. So a book on philosophy cannot ignore the idea. Most great philosophers did not. However, it treats the idea philosophically (by reason) rather than religiously (by faith). It is no part of this book either to presuppose or to try to prove or disprove religious faith, either overtly or as a "hidden agenda." I have tried to be equally fair to all points of view, including nihilism, skepticism, Marxism, and even Deconstructionism, which I cannot help suspecting is not even serious but just "jerking our chain."

# A Personal Bibliography

Please note: this is merely "*a* bibliography," one among many possible lists of recommended further reading, of other books I have written about these philosophers.

The very best books to read are, of course, the books of the great philosophers themselves, or the "great books." Why anyone would oppose "great books" blows my mind. Do they prefer tiny books, shallow books, or stupid books?

Most of the "great books" in the history of philosophy are surprisingly short and surprisingly clear, for they were written for intelligent, literate ordinary people, not for other philosophes. (This becomes increasingly rare as we approach the present time.) Seventeen of these classics are listed in the previous section, "A Very Short Introduction to Philosophy."

(1) Solomon: *Three Philosophies of Life* (Ignatius Press)

(2) Shankara: *Philosophy of Religion* (taped lectures, Recorded Books),

(3) Buddha, *op. cit.*

(4) Confucius, *op. cit.*

(5) Lao Tzu, *op. cit.*

(6) Presocratics, Greeks, and Moderns: *The Journey* (InterVarsity Press)

(7) Socrates: *Philosophy 101 by Socrates: an Introduction to Philosophy via Plato's "Apology"* (St. Augustine's Press)

(8) Plato: *The Platonic Tradition* (St. Augustine's Press)

(9) Plato: *Socrates' Student* (an introduction to Plato's *Republic*) (St. Augustine's Press)

(10) Aristotelian logic: *Socratic Logic* (St. Augustine's Press)

(11) Jesus: *The Philosophy of Jesus* (St. Augustine's Press)

(12) Jesus: *Socrates Meets Jesus* (InterVarsity Press)

(13) Jesus: *Jesus Shock* (St. Augustine's Press)

(14) Muhammad: *Between Allah and Jesus* (InterVarsity Press)

(15) Augustine: *I Burned for Your Peace* (Ignatius Press)

(16) Aquinas: *Summa of the Summa* (Ignatius Press)

(17) Aquinas, *A Shorter Summa* (Ignatius Press)

(18) Aquinas, an introduction (Recorded Books)

(19) Aquinas, *Practical Theology (Ignatius Press)*

(20) Machiavelli: *Socrates Meets Machivevlli* (St. Augustine's Press)

(21) Pascal: *Christianity for Modern Pagans: Pascal's "Pensees"* (Ignatius Press)

(22) Descartes: *Socrates Meets Descartes* (St. Augustine's Press)

(23) Hume: *Socrates Meets Hume* (St. Augustine's Press)

(24) Kant: *Socrates Meets Kant* (St. Augustine's Press)

(25) Marx: *Socrates Meets Marx* (St. Augustine's Press)

(26) Kierkegaard: *Socrates Meets Kierkegaard* (St. Augustine's Press)

(27) Freud: *Socrates Meets Freud* (St. Augustine's Press)

(28) Sartre: *Socrates Meets Sartre* (St. Augustine's Press)

(29) Modern philosophers argued with: *Summa Philosophica* (St. Augustine's Press)

(30) A history of ethics "What Would Socrates Do?" (Recorded Books)

# A Few Recommended Histories of Philosophy

Here are a selected few histories of philosophy which do not duplicate mine but have somewhat different ends.

(1) Frederick Copleston, S.J. has written the most clear and complete multi-volume history of Western philosophy available, with increasing detail and attention as it gets more and more contemporary. It is not exciting or dramatic or "existential" but it is very logical and helpful.

(2) Will Durant's *The Story of Philosophy* is charmingly and engagingly written, though very selective and very personally "angled."

(3) Bertrand Russell, a major philosopher himself, has written a very intelligent, very witty, history of Western philosophy from the viewpoint of a modern, "Enlightenment" atheist. Don't expect fair and equal treatment of both sides.

(4) Francis Parker's one-volume history of philosophy up to Hegel, *The Story of Western Philosophy,* centers on the theme of the one and the many.

(5) Mortimer Adler's *Ten Philosophical Mistakes* is not a complete history but a diagnostic treatment of key errors in modern philosophy.

(6) Etienne Gilson's *The Unity of Philosophical Experience* does the same.

(7) William Barrett's *Irrational Man,* though only an introduction to existentialism, has some very powerfully written and engaging historical chapter s on pre-existentialist philosophy from the existentialist viewpoint, as well as the best available one-chapter summaries of Kierkegaard, Nietzsche, Heidegger, and Sartre. His *The Illusion of Technique* thoughtfully compares James, Wittgenstein, and Heidegger.

Most philosophy texts today are anthologies of recent *articles* written by recent philosophers about recent systematic issues. Most of these are thin, dry, technical, dull, and lacking in "existential" bite, though all of them are very intelligent. They have their place. But usually, only Math and Science students, not English or History students, like them.

The very short "selected bibliographies" at the end of some chapters (only important ones) are for beginners, not scholars. They are chosen for readability, for their power to interest and move the reader.

# Introduction to Medieval Philosophy

## Its Relation to Religion

The most obvious difference between medieval philosophers and both the ancient philosophers before them and the modern philosophers after them is that medieval philosophers are also theologians. For them, philosophy is closely connected with religion (though not identical with it). More than that, for them the Christian religion is superior to philosophy because they believe it to be "divine revelation," i.e., originating not in man's mind but God's.

This does not mean that religious unbelievers cannot enter into dialog with them, for (1) they argue not only about religious issues but also about the same "secular" issues the Greeks did, and (2) because their method is often strictly philosophical rather than theological—that is, they appeal *not* to faith by assuming the truth of Christianity (or Judaism or Islam) as divine revelation, but often only to logic, universal human experience, and rational understanding.

Some medieval philosophers (e.g., Boethius, Aquinas, and Scotus) were very careful to distinguish between theological arguments (from premises accepted by religious faith) and philosophical arguments (from premises known by reason alone). Others (e.g., Augustine, Anselm, and Bonaventura), while aware of the distinction, were less concerned with it, and blended the two ways of thinking like the chocolate and vanilla parts of a marble cake.

If association with another enterprise pollutes philosophy, then modern philosophy is just as "polluted" as medieval, for it is typically as closely related to and in admiration of science as medieval philosophy is to religion, especially in method. Most modern philosophers assume that science* is the most prestigious and certain of human enterprises, just as most medieval philosophers assumed that religion is.

There is a religious assumption at the root of those who would dismiss medieval philosophy for being too religious. The very term "Middle Ages" was coined by the atheists of the French Revolution as an insult: the (bad) religious philosophers of the 1000 years in the "middle" between the (good) nonreligious philosophers of pre-Christian Greece and Rome and the (good) nonreligious philosophers of post-Christian Europe. Thus the assumption behind the insulting term "Middle Ages" is that the Christian

---

\*   I mean by "science" here modern science, especially the physical sciences, which use the scientific method. Premodern thinkers used the word "science" more broadly: the Greeks classified philosophy as a science and the medievals classified theology as a science

religion is false. (If it were true, it would be an *aid* to philosophy, for philosophy seeks the same thing, truth.) And the assumption that this religion is false is just as much a religious assumption (an assumption about religion) as the assumption that this religion is true.

### The Concepts "Ancient," "Medieval," and "Modern"

The traditional division of philosophy, and history, is into three eras—"ancient," "medieval," and "modern."*

This division has substantive, and not just conventional, reasons behind it. One of the most pervasive differences concerns the perspective from which everything is seen:

Ancient thought is cosmocentric;

Medieval thought is theocentric;

Modern thought is anthropocentric.

Nearly all cultures distinguish (some more sharply than others) (a) the ordered universe that we humans find ourselves in, (b) ourselves, human beings, and (c) a possible superhuman reality (Platonic Ideas, gods, or God). All three eras, ancient and medieval and modern, think about all three levels of reality, the sub-human, the human, and the super-human. But the ancients were cosmocentric because they classified men and gods by their place on the cosmic hierarchy; neither men nor gods were outside it. Medieval man was theocentric because he classified both nature and man as relative to the transcendent Creator-God; thus they used the word "the creation" instead of "the cosmos" and spoke of man as God's "creature." And moderns are anthropocentric because they tend to think about both the universe and God in terms of man; thus science is valued more for its practical payoff in making human life easier by technology than for its truth about the cosmos, and religion is valued more for its practical payoff in human happiness and moral goodness than for its truth about God.

### The Medieval Attitude to Greek Philosophy

Medieval philosophers inherited two traditions: Greek philosophy and Christian religion. How were these two to be related? Three answers emerged, and one prevailed. (1) Some saw Greek philosophy as a threat and enemy to religious faith. (2) Some virtually identified the two, or reinterpreted the religion to conform to the philosophy. (3) But most medievals, and all the great medieval philosophers until Ockham, saw them

---

*   Perhaps we should add a fourth, the "postmodern," and perhaps not, since (1) there is no clear consensus as to just what that term means, beyond "a crisis of reason," and (2) in many ways "postmodern" thinking is not anti-modern but hyper-modern, e.g., in its tendency to solipsism, subjectivism, skepticism (especially of metaphysics), and linguistic nihilism.

as distinct but complementary, like men and women, and they "married" or synthesized them.

Option #1 rejected philosophy for the sake of religion. Option #2 either rejected religion for the sake of philosophy (a rare and dangerous thing to do in the Middle Ages) or transformed the Christian religion by the standards of philosophy. Option #3 transformed philosophy by the standards of the Christian religion, and used philosophy for ultimately religious ends.

The first and most famous expression of this synthesis (Option #3) was the first chapter of John's Gospel, in which the author identifies the "Logos" (wisdom, order, law, meaning, intelligibility, mind, truth, reason, word—a term as deep and dense and diverse as the ocean) that was sought by the Greek philosophers with Christ as the incarnation of the Mind of God ("the Word became flesh"). Just as they argued to the Jews that Christ fulfilled all the Jewish prophecies, as the Messiah or "promised one," the Christians also argued to the pagan philosophers that Christ and His religion also fulfilled the philosophers' quest for wisdom and truth.

### The History of Philosophy as a Tree

Each of the four eras of the history of philosophy—ancient, medieval, modern, postmodern—contains more philosophers than the preceding era. Volume I of this book omitted only a few minor and unimportant Greek philosophers. Volume II omits more medievals, because there *are* more medievals, and there are even more moderns, and even more postmoderns or contemporaries. Today there are perhaps a million philosophers in the world, and not one of them is as obviously great or famous as Socrates, Plato, or Aristotle. Philosophers seem to diminish in greatness as they expand in number. (Are quality and quantity inversely proportionate?) The history of philosophy looks like a tree, with the Greeks as the few but supremely important roots, the medievals as the strong and simple trunk (there was more unity in medieval philosophy than in any other era), the moderns as many oppositely growing branches, and contemporaries as a plethora of little leaves on the branches.

### Augustine and Aquinas as the Two Medieval Giants

Augustine and Aquinas are the two undisputed giants of medieval philosophy, the two greatest Christian philosophers of all time. Augustine is often summarized as a Christianized Plato and Aquinas as a Christianized Aristotle, but this is much too simple, both because they were far more creative than that and because Aristotle himself is very Platonic. Thus Aquinas is very "Augustinian" (and thus "Platonic") as well as Aristotelian. He frequently quotes Augustine, almost never simply disagreeing with him. Yet their personalities are very different, as are their styles of philosophical writing. Augustine is a poet, Aquinas a logician. Augustine's thinking is concrete, personal, and existential; Aquinas's is abstract, impersonal, and essential. Augustine is passionately impatient to pierce through the world of human experience to reach God; Aquinas is dispassionately patient in mapping every step of the road, and careful to do justice to nature as well as the supernatural. Augustine philosophized with a passionate heart, Aquinas with an ordering mind.

# 34. St. John the Evangelist (6–100 A.D.?)

Of course St. John the Evangelist, youngest of Jesus' twelve apostles and author of the fourth Gospel (probably between 60 and 90 A.D.), was not a philosopher in the same sense as Aristotle, Aquinas, or Hegel (even though his Gospel is much more "philosophical" than the other three Gospels in terminology in probing deeper meanings). But neither was Thales, yet he is unanimously identified as the first ancient Greek philosopher because he began, in a very simple way, the radically new thing that was Western philosophy, in asking the question: What is everything? This was a quantum leap forward. So was St. John, who began, in the very simplest and most basic possible way, the medieval enterprise of Christian philosophy. In fact Thales, John, and Descartes were the three who each announced a radical new beginning for philosophy, a new *kind* of philosophy, one each for the three eras ancient, medieval and modern.*

Like Thales, John is important for a single sentence: the equation of the philosophers' Logos with Christ, and thus the beginning of the marriage between philosophical reason and religious faith. That is the new theme of all medieval philosophy.

All medieval philosophers in the West were Christians. All believed and assumed the truth of the Christian world-view—God, Creation, Incarnation, Resurrection, Last Judgment—as divine revelation, as a matter of religious faith. Some attempted to prove a few or many of the elements of this faith by philosophical reasoning, but this was another thing. The essence of Christianity is not a speculative philosophy but a religion, a faith, a trust, a personal relationship with God. Yet inherent in this religion are many momentous philosophical assumptions and even more momentous philosophical consequences.

The central one is the one John makes explicit for the first time in the first chapter of his Gospel: that the *Logos*, the ultimate Truth, Intelligibility, Meaning, Mind, Reason, Wisdom, or Word that was the goal sought by all the philosophers, existed from eternity as God, and became a man in Jesus Christ: **"the Logos was made flesh, and dwelt among us."** (St. Paul performed virtually the same identification between Christ and the philosophical notion of *Sophia* or wisdom: cf. I Cor. 1:24.)

---

* It could be reasonably said that all the history of philosophy is embryonically contained in three sentences. The first, uttered by Thales, the fount of Greek philosophy, is: **Everything is water**. This is the first attempt at a rational account of the universal, the absolute. The second is John's identification of this ultimate truth or "logos" with Christ; **the Logos became flesh**. This is the foundation of medieval philosophy. The third is Descartes's new psychological, humanistic, subjectivistic beginning to philosophy: **I think, therefore I am**.

When John wrote this equation—the Logos equals Jesus Christ—he was not Hellenizing Christianity and turning it into a rational philosophy, but Christianizing Hellenic philosophy at its very core. He was not turning Christ into Logos but Logos into Christ. Similarly, when St. Paul equated Christ with Wisdom (*Sophia*), he was not reducing Christ to abstract philosophical wisdom but claiming that the wisdom all the philosophers had sought was to be found in Christ, in its whole ontological reality, though the unpacking and exploration of this wisdom would take millennia.

This equation joined, at their very center, the two intellectual or spiritual traditions that most deeply formed subsequent Western civilization. All medieval philosophers, in some sense, worked at that enterprise, that marriage of religion and philosophy, faith and reason, in different ways. For some, it was a stormy marriage. Some doubted it should even be consummated. But most played midwife to it and helped it to produce fruit, philosophical children which were both children of Christ and children of Socrates.

# 35. St. Justin Martyr (ca. 114–180 A.D.)

Justin was not the first philosophical Christian, but he was the first Christian philosopher. The story of his conversion is so archetypical that it deserves a few paragraphs of telling. In the words of Etienne Gilson (in *The Spirit of Medieval Philosophy*):

> "St. Justin, in his *Dialogue with Trypho*, gives us a very living and picturesque account of his own conversion. The aim of philosophy, as he had always conceived it, is to bring us into union with God. (**"Do not all the philosophers turn every discourse on God?"**) Justin first made trial of a Stoic, but . . . he admitted that he did not regard the knowledge of God as indispensable. The Peripatetic [Aristotelian] who followed him began by insisting on an agreement about the fee for his lessons, an attitude that Justin did not regard as particularly worthy of a philosopher. The third professor was a Pythagorean, and he in turn soon bowed him out on the ground that Justin had not studied music, astronomy and geometry, all of them necessary preliminaries to any study of philosophy. A Platonist, who came next, did better. . . . 'The contemplation of the Ideas lent wings to my mind so that after a little time I seemed to myself to have become wise. I was even foolish enough to hope that I was about to look on God, such being the aim of the philosophy of Plato.' Everything was thus going on well when Justin fell in with a venerable old man, who, questioning him about God and the soul, showed that he was involved in strange contradictions. And when Justin inquired how he came by so much knowledge of these matters, he answered thus: 'In the most remote times, long before the day of any of these pretended philosophers, there lived certain men, happy, just and loved by God, who spoke by the Holy Spirit. . . . We call them prophets. . . . They did not deal in demonstrations, for far above all demonstrations they were worthy *witnesses* to the truth.' At these words the heart of Justin suddenly burned within him, and, says he, 'revolving all these things in my mind it seemed to me that here was the only sure and profitable philosophy. That is how and why I became a philosopher.'"

"A man (1) seeks the truth by the unaided effort of reason, and (2) is disappointed; (3) it is offered to him by faith, and he accepts; and (4) having accepted, he finds that it satisfies his reason." These are the four typical steps in intellectual conversions, and would be the pattern for Augustine's much more famous one. As Gilson summarizes it, "What he finds in Christianity, along with many other things, is the attainment of philosophic truths by non-philosophic methods."

Thinking about the metaphysical basis for this experience, Justin credits it to the universal Logos, and in ch. 10 of his *First Apology*, entitled "Christ compared with Socrates," he writes: **Whatever philosophers uttered well, they elaborated by finding and contemplating some part of the Logos. But since they did not know the whole of the Logos, which is Christ, they often contradicted themselves. . . . Socrates, who was more zealous in this direction than all of them, was accused of the very same crimes as ourselves . . . (but) no one trusted in Socrates so as to die for this doctrine, but in Christ, who was partially known even by Socrates, for He was and is the Logos who is in every man (Jn 1:9).**

It is all very simple and direct and personal and religious, rather than philosophically subtle and elaborate; but this is the foundation for all subsequent medieval philosophy.

# 36. St. Augustine (354–430)

In the entire history of the world, there may have been some greater philosophical and theological mind than Augustine, but I don't know who that could possibly be, except Thomas Aquinas; and there may have been a more passionate and beautiful philosophical poet, though I don't know who that could possibly be at all; but there has certainly never been anyone greater than Augustine in both respects. These two qualities, extremities of head and heart, which can tear lesser souls in two, united Augustine's. Medieval statuary always has him holding an open book in one hand and a burning heart in the other. Whether the heart is meant to be his own or God's, I do not know: that's how similar they are. (That's what makes him a saint.)

Paradoxically, it is the very uniqueness of Augustine's double passion that makes him Everyman writ large. For heart and mind are the two deepest powers in everyone, especially if it is true, as Augustine believed, that we are made in the image of a God who is infinite Truth and infinite Love.

For Augustine, truth and love, mind and heart, are absolute values, but the heart is the deepest. "Heart" in Augustine, as in Scripture, means not sentiment or emotion but love. He writes: **"Amor meus, pondus meum"—"my love is my gravity,"** my weight, my destiny. I go where my love draws me—ultimately to God or no-God, Heaven or Hell, life or death, light or darkness, being or nonbeing.

Every person alive in Western civilization would be a very different person today if Augustine had not lived. No one outside the Bible ever had more influence on the history of Western civilization, except perhaps Socrates. For Augustine, more than anyone else, defined the main line of the medieval mind, the marriage or synthesis of faith and reason, of Christianity and classical culture, especially Greek philosophy—in other words, Jesus and Socrates, the two most influential persons who ever lived.

The most fundamental reason for the crisis of Western civilization today is that this synthesis, the marriage brokered by the medievals and set in motion by Augustine more than any one other person, is in crisis. Three crises above all define our present culture: of faith, of reason, and of the marriage between them. The first point is admitted even by agnostics like William Barrett, in *Irrational Man* (the best survey of Existentialism ever written), who says that *"the most important feature of modern civilization is unquestionably the decline of religion."* And the second point is clear from a study of modern philosophy; for if there is one central theme in modern philosophy, from Ockham to Derrida, it is the crisis of reason, and the decline of faith in reason. Therefore, to understand ourselves, we need to study Augustine, at least for contrast.

He lived during the troubled times of the end of one age (the ancient classical age, the dying Roman Empire) and the beginning of another (medieval Christendom). He lived through the world-shakingly traumatic Fall of Rome in 410 A.D. and died as the smoke and fires of the barbarians were burning his North African town.*

Rome had been not just a city but "the eternal city," civilization itself, seemingly indestructible. Once and once only was the Western world politically and culturally united, and now this civilization—civilization itself, it seemed—was dying. The contemporary equivalent would be a "nuclear winter." The "Dark Ages" were descending on the world for the next 500 years.

To such a powerful crisis Augustine responded by doing one of the most powerful things a man can do: he wrote a book—in fact many books, but two in particular, two of the most influential books ever written, the *Confessions* and *The City of God.*

The 1500–page *City of God* is the world's first philosophy of history. It interprets all of human history, from the Creation to the Last Judgment, as the drama of divine providence and human free choice (both of which Augustine strongly defended), centering on the choice between the two most fundamental options of human life: membership in one or the other of the two "cities." (He defined a "**city**" as "**an association of men bound by a common love.**") "**The City of God**" (*Civitas Dei*) is the invisible community of all who love God as God, and "**the City of the World**" (*Civitas Mundi*) is all those who love the world and themselves as their God. "**Two loves have made two cities.**" The central plot of the drama of human history is the conflict and interplay of these two cities, which culminate in Heaven and Hell. (What could be more dramatic than that?)

Augustine's other masterpiece, the *Confessions,* is the very same drama in Augustine's own life. It is the most popular Christian book in history next to the Bible, and on its first page we find the most famous Christian sentence outside the Bible, which summarizes both this book and the central meaning of every human life: "**Thou hast made us for Thyself, and [therefore] our hearts are restless until they rest in Thee.**"

This book's power comes from its passionate, searing, Job-like honesty, for it is written to the all-knowing *God*; we human readers are only eavesdroppers. Like *Job* it is apparently the story of man's search for God but really the story of God's search for man. It contains more interrogative sentences than any other great book not written in a literal dialog format. Augustine was simply incapable of fudging or dodging a question.

When Pascal, twelve centuries later, knew he was dying, he gave away all his books

---

\* Augustine was born in Thagaste, North Africa (part of the Roman Empire) and later became the Bishop of Hippo. St. Francis of Assisi may have been a preacher to the birds but St. Augustine was a Bishop to a Hippo.

except the Bible and the *Confessions.* ("A wise choice," comments Malcolm Muggeridge.) They were the two main sources for Pascal's own little masterpiece, the *Pensées.*

No one should be allowed to die without having read the *Confessions.* It is the world's first spiritual (and philosophical) autobiography, and by far the most famous. It is astonishingly contemporary. There is nothing even remotely like it in pre-modern literature for introspective depth and passion. If you read it, be sure to read it in Frank Sheed's powerful singing translation. (Hackett publ.) Read it slowly. Taste it on the tongue and in the stomach. Hear it in the ear and in the heart. Chew it like gum rather than swallowing it like a pill. It sings. It cries. It shouts. It bleeds. It whispers. It stands silent and amazed. So do you if you dare to enter it.

There is too much in the *Confessions* for anything but a pitifully lame summary here. There is passion, profundity, practical psychology, sin, sex (they are *not* identified with each other!), saintliness, mysticism, and logic, for starters.

A third masterpiece, *On the Trinity,* is the foundational philosophical-theological work about the primary, centrally distinctive doctrine in Christianity. It is also the first source of modern personalism, by clearly distinguishing "person" and "nature" and by defining a "person," human or divine, not merely in terms of substance but in terms of relations. (See Paul Henry, S.J., *St. Augustine on Personality,* and W. Norris Clarke, S.J., *Person and Being.*)

Augustine wrote these three books in response to three crises. *On the Trinity* was his response to errors about the central doctrine of Christian theology (and, if true, the ultimate nature of reality). *The City of God* was his response to the fall of Rome, that is, of civilization itself. The *Confessions* was his response to the greatest crisis of all, the identity crisis each of us is born with, the central drama of time whose end is eternal success or eternal failure.

### The Search for the Summum Bonum

Augustine's philosophy is dramatic and "existential" (personal), and therefore the best way to summarize it is dramatically and existentially, in a "big picture." Let us begin by asking the Socratic question, "Know thyself." This meant for Socrates not merely "Discover your unique individual talents, desires, personality, and happiness" but "Discover the universal human situation, the 'meaning of life,' and the laws of human nature." Augustine's strikingly un-Socratic answer to this Socratic question is that without God man is a living tragedy. (Book 19 of *The City of God* is a good example to sample.)

Man is essentially a seeker, a lover, a desirer. He needs to discover and attain his own end and home and happiness. (No word moves us more deeply than the word "home"—that was the whole arresting charm of "E.T.") But he cannot! He is an orphan, a perpetual wanderer.

27

Four possible candidates appear for his home: nature below him, self within him, others around him, and God above him.

Like the animals, man is a creature of nature. But unlike them, he does not feel wholly at home in nature. It is beautiful, but it is home only to his body, not his soul. It limits him, thwarts him, and at best gives him only little appetizers of the things he wants without limit: truth, goodness, and beauty. Nature gives him pain, disease, old age, and death. In these pains we are born, in them we live, and in them we die.

But what of human love and society and culture? Nature may oppose us, but we have transcended it with family and friendship, culture and civilization, art and science, language and literature, law and order. We have made a home in the wilderness.

This is higher than nature but it is still not home for us. For the limitations of nature—especially its mortality—also infect all our human constructions in it. And this distinctively human dimension, while adding greater goods, also adds greater pains and evils: not just sufferings but sins, not just physical evils but moral evils: lies, betrayals, injustices, hatreds. Our history is one long war. Not only nature but also culture disappoints us. It is necessary, but it is not home.

But what of the inner life of the individual soul? We find here high ideals, aspirations for Truth and Goodness and Beauty that tell us that these things are real and that they are our destiny.

But there is a terrible chasm between our awareness of them and our ability to attain them, between the ideal and the reality. We betray these ideals as much as society does, for society is nothing but ourselves acting together. Only fools think they are wise; only sinners think they are saints, and only pitifully vain and ugly souls think they are beautiful. When we look honestly at ourselves we find not only wisdom and unselfish love, but we also find that we are stupid, selfish, lustful, and violent. We betray our own ideals. "We have met the enemy and he is us."

If there is any hope, then, it must come from a God who is free of all these natural and human imperfections. And the vast majority of people in history have believed in a God or gods. But His very perfection makes Him incapable of being found by the likes of us. If we cannot even find the natural happiness we long for, how could we find our way to supernatural perfection?

The classical Greeks knew that man transcended nature, and sought happiness in society. The Stoics and Epicureans lost that faith and turned to their own souls and bodies. Most people turned to popular religion. But Augustine found the enemy here too, in fact here above all. Even our natural (pagan) religions are infected with our own sins, which we project onto our gods. They are arbitrary and selfish beings like ourselves. They need us as much as we need them. And they do not love us.

Our only hope is that a perfect God who does not need us nevertheless loves us and saves us from ourselves. All human ways up fail; our only hope is a divine way down. And this is the Christian key that Augustine inserts into the human lock. And he explores the human lock, especially in the *Confessions* and *The City of God*, with as much passion and detail as he explores the divine key—which explains his universal appeal even to those who do not believe in his religious key.

## Faith and Reason

Augustine says there are two guides to truth: human reason and faith.

"Faith" is not a subjective feeling or opinion that arises within us; it is our affirmative response to objective divine revelation. And divine revelation centers and culminates in Christ, who is also the eternal Logos, truth, or divine intelligence which designed and created us and in which human reason participates. So both guides to truth, faith and reason, are from and for Christ.

As with St. Justin Martyr, the key to perfecting reason (wisdom, understanding) is faith. Augustine loves to quote Isaiah 7:9: ***"Unless you believe, you will not understand"***—the ideal St. Anselm would make famous in the motto ***"fides quaerens intellectum,"*** "faith seeking understanding."

Augustine is thinking of knowing *God* here, not just knowing abstract *ideas*; and God is three *Persons*; and the only way to deeply understand a person, human or divine, is by loving and trusting, i.e., by faith. The ultimate motive and goal of Augustine's philosophizing is not to solve intellectual puzzles but to know God, to see God. Augustine had a profoundly philosophical mind, yet he never thought of creating a philosophy for its own sake; it was inseparable from religion.

It is a mistake to look in Augustine for the clear distinction between philosophy and theology, or between reason and faith, that are found in later thinkers like Boethius and Aquinas. It is equally a mistake to say that Augustine did not know the difference between them. He used both at once because both are ways to wisdom, and he was so passionately pointed toward their common end (wisdom) that he did not linger over mapping the differences between the means. Nor was he concerned to clearly distinguish the different divisions of philosophy itself (logic, epistemology, metaphysics, anthropology, ethics, etc.).

Above all other philosophers Augustine loved Plato (actually the Neo-Platonists; he probably never read Plato himself). Some claim that he Platonized Christianity. Others say he Christianized Plato, or "baptized" Plato. Still others say he "married" or "synthesized" Plato and Christianity. Aquinas summarized his relationship to Plato most clearly and simply when he wrote: **Whenever Augustine, who was imbued with the doctrines of the Platonists, found in their writings anything consistent with the faith, he adopted it, and whatever he found contrary to the faith, he amended.** (Aquinas's words apply equally to Aquinas's own relationship to Aristotle.) Augustine had the instincts of a sailor: he negotiated the heavy seas of Platonism in the Christian boat without capsizing. To put the point without an analogy, he was just about the only major early Christian theologian in the West who consistently avoided both the simple rejection of

Plato as a heretic and the skewering of Christianity in a Platonic direction so as to become somewhat of a heretic himself.

## Augustine's Epistemology

(1) The problem of certitude loomed large for the early Augustine, for he had been a skeptic himself. Skepticism flourished in the late Platonic Academy, so that in Augustine's day, as in ours, an "academic" was almost a synonym for a skeptic. *Against the Academics (Contra Academicos)* is his refutation of skepticism; and Descartes, "the father of modern philosophy," used many of its ideas, especially the argument **"I doubt, therefore I am"**—but Augustine never tried to construct a whole philosophical system on this foundation, as Descartes did.

(a) One of the skeptics' arguments is from optical illusions and the untrustworthiness of the senses. Augustine replies that even if sensory appearances distort reality, we are certain that the appearances appear to our consciousness. We may judge wrongly that a stick held in the water is really broken (an optical illusion), but we do see that it appears broken. It is the mind, not the senses, that misleads us.

(b) The senses, however, do not give us certainty, but the mind does. We are in fact all certain that we exist and that we think, even if we think wrongly about everything else. (This is the origin of Descartes's "I think, therefore I am.")

(c) We find other certain truths in our minds, e.g., mathematical truths like $3+7=10$, which cannot change and do not depend on the senses or the material world. We also find moral truths, e.g., that an eternal good is better than a temporal good. How can we explain the presence of such certain knowledge of unchangeable truth in our souls?

It cannot be caused by changing sensible things, for the contingent cannot cause the necessary. Nor can our own minds be their source, for our minds too are changing and contingent and fallible. Our mind discovers and submits to and is ruled by truth rather than creating it. And different minds see the same truths. Augustine asks: **When you and I both see the same truth [e.g., that $3+7=10$], where do we see it? You do not see it in me nor do I see it in you, but both of us see it in itself, in the truth that transcends both of us.** We discover immutable, necessary, and eternal truth above the human mind.

(d) The only being that possesses these attributes is God. Thus discovering truth is discovering God, and proving the existence of truth is proving the existence of God, however "thin" this God is, i.e., however inadequately we may understand what "God" means. Obviously this is not a proof of all that the Bible means by "God." But it is enough to refute atheism.

The method is typical of Augustine. It is Platonically intellectual and inward rather than Aristotelianly empirical and outward. It leads upward via inward, **from the exterior to the interior and from the inferior to the superior.**

(2) Augustine accepted Plato's Theory of Ideas but gave them a home in the Mind of God. He explained our knowledge of eternal truths by **"divine illumination"** rather

than by Plato's doctrine of reincarnation and the "recollection" (*anamnesis*) of innate ideas. Whenever anyone makes a true judgment, his mind is in contact with these divine Ideas, though they themselves are not seen, like the sun behind our heads. He loves to quote the scripture: "*In thy light we see light.*" This is not a special or mystical illumination but a natural and universal one. As the eye receives sensible light from the creation, the mind receives intelligible light from the Creator, from the Logos, the Word or Mind of God which "*lightens every man who comes into the world*" (John 1:9). That is why there is in all men **the light of eternal reason, in which light the immutable truths are seen.**

(3) Augustine explains *sensation* in a curious way. It is not by Aristotle's doctrine of abstraction of universal forms from material things, since Augustine argues that the inferior (bodies) cannot impress their images on the superior (the spiritual soul, or mind). Matter cannot act on spirit. Thus sensation is an act of the soul's "vital attention." **It is not the body that impresses the image in our soul. It is the soul itself that produces it with wonderful swiftness within itself.**

### Augustine's Anthropology

(1) Augustine, unlike Plotinus, believes that man is body *and* soul, that the body is part of human nature, and he does not say that the body is evil or the source of evil. As a Christian he believes that matter and the body is good and created by God. Since God created all that is, **all that is, is good.**

But he sees the soul as the true center, the self itself, the *I*, the personality. He defines man as **a rational soul using a mortal body.** The center of the self is the soul; the body is its instrument.

And though both are good, the soul is better than the body. Yet our souls usually care more for the body and bodily goods than for themselves and spiritual goods, and that foolishness and addiction is its prison and its burden. Thus the body, *and* the soul, and man himself, are essentially good, ontologically good, but practically and morally fallen into evil. The distinction is easy to overlook. Augustine is passionate and uncompromising about the ontological good as well as the moral evil.

(Yet he retains a Platonic view of the dualism of body and soul. An instructive example of theological progress would be the comparison between Augustine's Platonic view of the body and John Paul II's much more positive "Theology of the Body." The latter is a progress and a corrective to, yet continuous with, and dependent on, most of Augustine's insights.)

(2) Soul and body do not make a single substance for Augustine, as they do for Aristotle and Aquinas. The soul is a substance by itself, and is united with the body in the same way the mind is united with the senses: by "vital attention."

(3) God and the soul are his only two absolute concerns. **I desire to know God and the soul. Nothing more? Nothing whatever.** For God and himself are the only two realities he will never be able to escape at any time or in eternity. To know them is so important to him that everything else is either a means to that end or simply not important. Augustine's thought is not dispassionate, like a scientist's, but passionate, like a lover's, and therefore it comes to a point rather than being "well-rounded."

## Augustine's Theology and Metaphysics

(1) Because of "Divine Illumination," God is *present* to our minds as well as above us and ruling our minds. He is both immanent and transcendent.

(2) He is indefinable. We know *that* He is but not *what* He is. We know only what He is not. In fact, we know Him best as that which transcends our knowledge. He is not only superior to our minds but superior to everything. He is **that to which nothing can be known to be superior.** (Later, St. Anselm, Augustine's faithful disciple, will use this negative definition of God, reworded as **that than which nothing greater can be conceived,** in his famous "ontological argument" for God's existence. See ch. 40.)

(3) The best name for God is the one He Himself revealed to us, to Moses in the burning bush (Exodus 3:14): **I AM**. God is Being itself (*ipsum esse)*.

(4) But what does *"being"* mean? True being, says Augustine, means eternal being, rather than becoming; being that is unmixed with the non-being of past (which is the non-being of no-longer) and future (which is the non-being of not-yet). Most of our being, in time, is no longer or not yet; we are being spilled out onto time's, like a bucket of water spilled out onto a floor.

(What a philosopher means by "being" is the most abstract yet important and consequential question of his metaphysics. Parmenides and Shankara meant oneness, Plato meant essentially "intelligibility," Augustine "eternity," and Aquinas "actual existence." See Gilson, *Being and Some Philosophers* on this very difficult question.)

(5) When Augustine thinks about *time,* he confronts this puzzle: Think of time as a line and the present moment as a point on that line. If the present is merely the extensionless point dividing the past from the future; and if the past, no matter how long its line may have been, *is* no longer; and if the future, no matter how long its line will be, is not yet; then being in time has no "size" or "length" at all!

Better to think of the present as including rather than excluding the past and the future. The past (i.e., the pastness of the past) is made by memory, made only in the present, which is the only real moment of time; and similarly, the future is made only by our anticipation, which is also present. Thus time is not merely objective and physical but also subjective and mental. Our minds make time! (Kant would later use this notion, not just for time but also for all categories or forms: see ch. 67.)

For God, there is only *eternity*, which means not time-without-end but *simultaneity*. Everything that to us was or will be exists for God at once in a timeless present. Our temporal thinking shatters that eternal unity and sees things piecemeal. (There may be a clue that Augustine was onto something real here in the fact that many people, at the moment of death, see their entire lives this way, all together at once in a single moment, yet with everything in its proper place.)

## Augustine's Cosmology

(1) Though he wants to know **only God and the soul, nothing more,** Augustine thinks deeply about creation and the cosmos too, since knowing the Creator and knowing the creation supplement each other. But Augustine is not interested in knowing the creation for its own sake. The constant movement of his thought is to God, not to the cosmos. The whole world to him is a series of pointing fingers, and he does not mistake the finger for the heavenly body it points to. He looks-along the world rather than looking-at it, like reading a text. In fact his medieval disciples often repeated the saying that nature was a second scripture, a book of signs written by God in things and events rather than words. Only a dog or a baby tries to play with a book, or eat it; a wise man *reads* it. This cosmology of things as signs or symbols actually gives the world *more* importance, not less, as a book is more important than a stone to a wise man.

(2) Augustine's Platonism lets him see all the perfections in the material and temporal world as reflections of immaterial and timeless Platonic Ideas. And since Augustine gives the Platonic Ideas a home in the Mind of God, this way of seeing the world becomes a way of knowing God, knowing the mind of the Artist through the matter of His art.

Later medieval philosophers would puzzle over two problems about the divine Ideas: how to reconcile the manyness of the divine Ideas with the oneness of God, and whether the Ideas were creatures or the Creator. These are the only two possible categories for a theist; but the Ideas apparently could not be creatures because they were eternal, and they could not be the Creator because they were many.

In the eighth century, the Irish Platonic philosopher John Scotus Erigena (ch. 39), in *The Division of Nature,* distinguished (1) "nature which creates and is not created" (God as Creator of all things), (2) "nature which is created and which creates" (the divine Ideas), (3) "nature which is created and does not create" (individual things), and (4) "nature which does not create and is not created" (God considered not as the Creator but as the final end of all things). The idea did not "catch on."

(3) Since God created the universe by a deliberate free choice and not by necessity (as in Plotinus), the question arises: Why? What was His reason or motive? Augustine's

answer is that it could only be purely unselfish love, to share His goodness not only within Himself, among the three Persons of the Trinity, but also with persons, and even things, that are not Himself.

(4) Creation is **"*ex nihilo,*"** out of nothing. Unlike Plato's or Aristotle's God, Augustine's God did not merely impose form and order on matter and chaos, but created matter itself. Therefore matter is good, not evil or the source of evil, as it was for Plotinus and the Manichees.

(5) Because the world was created, time is limited. The amount of past time is finite. The world is not co-eternal with God, as it is for Plato and Aristotle. Time is itself a creature, it is co-created with matter, ontologically relative to matter. (This is closer to Einstein than to Newton.) Since the world was not created *in* time, there was no time before creation.

(6) God did not create everything at once, nor did He miraculously intervene to create each new species, but created most things indirectly, in the form of "rational seeds" (*rationes seminales*) or planned potentialities that lie dormant in other things and which unfold and emerge gradually—a primitive notion of cosmic evolution.

The important theological principle here is that God generously shares His power with "second causes" and gives them the power to act in their own natural order, rather than "hogging the whole show" Himself. As later theologians like Aquinas state the principle, "grace perfects nature rather than demeaning it."

Augustine clearly states this general principle, but does not do justice to it everywhere, for he sometimes tries to promote God's glory by demoting that of creatures, e.g., in his epistemology of divine illumination rather than human abstraction as the source of our knowledge of Forms, and tries to promote the primacy of the soul by demoting the importance of the body, e.g., in his account of sensation as incapable of informing the mind from "below." This is a *practical* and necessary corrective to the opposite error of "hard empiricism" and materialism, which is much more common, but it makes for an inadequate philosophical *theory*. Augustine is much more concerned with the practical than with the theoretical.

## Augustine's Ethics

(1) Like Aristotle, Augustine centers his ethics on the center, the ***summum bonum,*** greatest good, final end, ultimate purpose, or meaning of life. Like Aristotle, he identifies it as **happiness**.

But his definition of happiness is not merely Aristotle's "active life of the soul according to all the virtues in a complete life" (though he does not deny this) but as "**joy in truth.**" These are the two things everyone wants—happiness and truth—always and infinitely, as the two things everyone wants to avoid are misery and ignorance.

(2) That is why in Augustine's ethics everything is relative to and leads to God: because God *is* truth and joy.

("Truth" for Augustine does not mean merely logical correctness, or the correspondence between a thought and a fact. It means [non-material] *light*. It is almost a substantial thing. It is the very life and food of the soul.)

Compared with more systematic thinkers like Aristotle or Aquinas, Augustine seems less orderly, even rambling. This is an illusion. His thought is very tightly ordered: to the one single end of God. It is the order of a hunter passionately seeking his one prey from every angle, circling around it in tightening spirals rather than straight lines. It is not the order of a map-maker mapping the whole territory objectively and impersonally from above. It is the order of the heart. Augustine's thought is unified by love, as man's life ought to be unified by love.

(3) And the ultimate reason for that is because God Himself, man's ultimate Good, is unified by love. It is love which makes the three Persons of the Trinity one. That is why the force that brings man to God is love. For love is both the essence of God and the essential thing in man. Love is the very heart and center of the human soul, in Augustine's anthropology.

Love is spiritual gravity. As Augustine puts it in a dense and profound analogy, **my love is my weight (*amor meus, pondus meum*).** We go where our loves draw us. Ultimately, all loves lead either to God (light and joy) or away from God (into darkness and misery). Our love is our destiny.

(4) Augustine knew vividly, from personal experience, that our life is a warfare between two loves: of good and evil, light and darkness; and that to be good we need not just reason and will and virtue but God's grace. (The *Confessions* could be seen as a commentary on Romans 7:15.) For we are broken, unnaturally divided: (a) the body is so divided from the soul that it separates from the soul and dies; (b) the passions are so divided from reason that they overcome it (as Plato thought was impossible); and (c) our very will, which was meant to obey reason and use passion, does the reverse because it is itself divided. (Romans 7:17; *Confessions*, bk. 8.)

(5) Therefore we lack freedom (liberty, *libertas*), even though we have free will (free choice, *liberum arbitrium*). We are addicts, sinaholics. Sin is slavery (Jn 8:34); true liberty would be sinlessness. We need a moral as well as an intellectual "divine illumination."

(6) This illumination and grace shines in our conscience, which is still vividly aware, even in its fallen state, of a "natural (moral) law," i.e., a law (a) *for* human nature that is also (b) known *by* human nature (natural reason, conscience). Conscience, after all, is not just a power of *feeling* but of *knowing*.

(7) This natural law, which reflects the eternal and unchangeable law in God's own will, mind, and nature, demands that the lower be obedient to the higher: man to God in reality, body to soul in man, passions to reason in the soul. Sin reverses this natural order.

(8) All sin is "disordered love." Virtue is **ordo amoris,** "the order of love," love ordered to its right object. Thus Augustine's famous saying **Love God and then do what you will.** For if you love God you will love His moral will. Augustine's ethics is as centered and unified and simple as its ultimate object, God Himself.

(9) God's grace is not external; it actually changes and re-orders the soul and its loves, so that **God becomes the life of the soul as the soul is the life of the body.** This begins now and is perfected in Heaven; in fact if it does not begin now, the soul could not endure Heaven.

### Augustine's Philosophy of History and Politics

Augustine's ethics and politics are mirror images of each other, as are his two masterpieces the *Confessions* and *The City of God.* Love is the center of both.

(1) The essence of the 1000+ page book *The City of God* is very simple: **Two loves have made two cities. Love of God to the refusal of self has made the City of God (*Civitas Dei*). Love of self to the refusal of God has made the City of the World (*Civitas Mundi*).** ("World" in Augustine, as in the New Testament, does not mean nature or earth or matter, which are God's good creations, but man's sinful nature, societies, and history.) The theme and plot of *The City of God* is the story of all of human history as the invisible spiritual warfare between these two cities. (That is also the theme and plot of the Bible.)

(2) The concept of a "city" (*civitas*) is at the heart of Augustine's political philosophy. (My college philosophy professor's final exam on Augustine consisted of just one word written on the blackboard: "civitas." He simply said: "Write on that.") A "city" is a "community" of men—literally a "common-unity"; but what makes it one? Love. **A city is a community of rational beings united by a single agreement about that which they love.** For societies as well as individuals, love is their destiny and their gravity. "Amor meus, pondus meum": we are what we love, our love makes our identity and our destiny.

(3) Here, then, is Augustine's mirror to know yourself and your deepest identity: **Let a man ask himself what he loves, and he will find what city he is a member of.** What he loves most is either God or an idol, which is anything other than God: any creature, yourself, others, or things in the world loved and worshipped as God, made into the *summum bonum.* This is simply the implicit meaning of Christ's "first and greatest commandment" (Mt. 22:37–38).

In a sermon on the love of God, Augustine asks us to make the following thought-experiment: Imagine God offering the following "deal": "I will give you anything you desire. Nothing will be impossible for you, nothing forbidden, and nothing punished, ever. But you will never see My face." Would you take that "deal"? If not, you are a member of the City of God; if so, you are a member of the other city.

(4) The two cities are real but invisible. They are not synonymous with the visible Church and the visible Roman Empire. Augustine's political point is not the distinction between church and state but between good and evil, and ultimately between Heaven and Hell. Though confused and mingled in this life, since there is some good in evil men and some evil in good men, the two cities will be clearly separated at the end of time, when their membership, and their eternal destinies in Heaven or Hell, will be revealed at the Last Judgment. While they are in time, Christians live, mingle, and cooperate with pagans in the secular city and work for its welfare as good citizens. Again, this is just the New Testament, interpreted philosophically. St. Thomas More's last words, before being martyred, reflect it: "I die the King's good servant, but God's first."

(5) This helps Augustine answer the pagan accusation that Christianity caused the Fall of Rome in 410 A.D., by (a) teaching detachment from the world and the state, (b) weakening patriotism by forgiving enemies, and (c) refusing to worship Rome's gods, who then punished Rome for its conversion to Christianity.

(6) After answering these charges in the first part, Augustine gets to his main point in the second: the history of the two cities. The City of God is the ultimate reason for the creation of the universe; for the universe is not immortal, but the City of God is. The universe is its womb, or its cradle.

Augustine had an enormous influence on the next 1000 years. *The City of God* and the *Confessions* were the two most popular books (other than the Bible) throughout the Middle Ages. *The City of God* inspired Christians to organize the earth into a secular city that took its principles from the sacred city and was made in its image as Man was made in God's image.

Augustine and Aquinas are unquestionably the two all-time giants of Christian thought, as Plato and Aristotle are of Greek thought. The parallel can be put in various ways: We can say (1) that Augustine "baptized" (Christianized) Plato and Aquinas "baptized" Aristotle; or (2) that the first half of Aristotle is Plato and the first half of Aquinas is Augustine; or (3) that as Aristotle stands on the shoulders of Plato, Aquinas stands on the shoulders of Augustine; or (4) that Aristotle is a Platonist Plus and Aquinas is an Augustinian Plus; or (5) that as Aristotle was the leafy branches of the tree of Greek philosophy, Plato the trunk, and Socrates the root, so in Christian thought Aquinas was the branches, Augustine the trunk, and Christ the root.

Some memorable quotations from the *Confessions* (to inveigle you to read the rest of it):

**(1) Thou hast made us for Thyself, and our hearts are restless till they rest in Thee.**

**(2) The one thing I delighted in was play, and for this I was punished by men who after all were doing exactly the same things themselves. But the idling of men is called business.**

**(3) Free curiosity is of more value in learning than harsh discipline.**

**(4) Even that I exist is Thy gift.**

**(5) Someone cries, "Come on, let's do it"—and we would be ashamed to be ashamed.**

**(6) I sought some object to love since I was in love with loving.**

**(7) Love and seek and win and hold and embrace not this or that philosophical school but Wisdom itself, whatever it might be.**

**(8)** (on the death of a dear friend:) **I had no delight but in tears, for tears had taken the place my friend had held in the love of my heart.**

**(9) I wondered that other mortals should live when he was dead whom I had loved as if he would never die; and I marveled still more that he should be dead and I his other self living still. . . . And it may be that I feared to die lest thereby he should die wholly.**

**(10) Where was my heart to flee for refuge from my heart?**

**(11) Surely a man is unhappy even if he knows all these things but does not know You; and that man is happy who knows You even though he knows nothing of them; and the man who knows both You and them is not the happier for them but only for You.**

**(12) My mind was in search of such images as the forms my eye was accustomed to see, and I did not realize that the mental act by which I formed these images was not itself a bodily image.**

**(13) I sought for the origin of evil, but I sought in an evil manner.**

(14) (on evil:) **Can it be that it is wholly without being? But why should we fear and be on guard against what is not? Or if our fear of it is groundless, then our very fear is itself an evil thing. For by it the heart is driven and tormented for no cause; and that evil is all the worse if there is nothing to fear yet we do fear. Thus either there is evil which we fear, or the fact that we fear is evil.**

(15) **Corruptible things are good: if they were supremely good they could not be corrupted, but also if they were not good at all they could not be corrupted ... for corruption damages, and unless it damaged goodness, it would not damage. . . . Thus whatsoever things are, are good; and that evil whose origin I sought is not a substance because if it were a substance it would be good.**

(16) **There is no sanity in those whom anything in creation displeases.**

(17) (on the Incarnation:) **He built for Himself here below a lowly house of our clay, that by it He might bring (mankind) down from themselves and up to Himself ... to the end that weary at last they might cast themselves down upon His humanity and rise again in its rising.**

(18) **But You, Lord, turned me back towards myself, taking me from behind my own back where I had put myself all the time that I preferred not to see myself. But there was no way to flee from myself.**

(19) **I had begged You for chastity, saying: "Grant me chastity and continence, but not yet." For I was afraid that You would hear my prayer too soon.**

(20) **The mind gives the body an order and is obeyed at once; the mind gives itself an order and is resisted. The mind commands the hand to move and there is such readiness that you can hardly distinguish the command from its execution. Yet the mind is mind, whereas the hand is body. The mind commands the mind to will; the mind is itself, but it does not do it. Why this monstrousness? And what is the root of it?**

(21) **Even if I would not confess to You, what could be hidden in me, O Lord, to whose eyes the deepest depth of man's conscience lies bare? I would only be hiding You from myself, not myself from You.**

(22) **Men are a race curious to know of other men's lives, but slothful to correct their own. Why should they wish to hear from me what I am, when they do not wish to hear from You what they are themselves?. . . . They have not their ear at my heart, where I am what I am.**

**(23) But what is it that I love when I love You?**

**(24) They love truth when it reveals itself and hate it when it reveals them. Thus it shall reward them as they deserve: those who do not wish to be revealed by truth, truth will unmask against their will, but it will not reveal itself to them. Thus does the human mind . . . desire to keep itself concealed, yet desire that nothing should be concealed from itself. But the contrary happens to it—it cannot lie hidden from truth, but only truth from it.**

**(25) Late have I loved thee, O Beauty so ancient and so new; late have I loved Thee. For behold Thou wert within me and I outside. And I sought Thee outside, and in my unloveliness fell upon those lovely things that Thou hast made. Thou wert with me and I was not with Thee. I was kept from Thee by those things, yet had they not been in Thee, they would not have been at all. Thou didst call and cry to me and burst open my deafness; Thou didst send forth Thy beams and shine upon me and chase away my blindness; Thou didst breathe fragrance upon me, and I drew in my breath and do now pant for Thee; I tasted Thee, and now hunger and thirst for Thee; Thou has touched me, and I have burned for Thy peace.**

### Selected Bibliography:

*St. Augustine and His Influence through the Ages* by Henri Marrou
*A Monument to St. Augustine* by Christopher Dawson
*The Christian Philosophy of St. Augustine* by Etienne Gilson
*The Conversion of Augustine* by Romano Guardini
*Son of Tears: A Novel of St. Augustine* by Henry Coray
*A Monument to St. Augustine* (anthology of essays)
*St. Augustine on Personality* by Paul Henry, S.J.

# 37. Boethius (480–524)

Boethius lived in the Western (Roman) Empire in troubled times, almost a century after Augustine and the Fall of Rome. The Empire was ruled by Theodoric and other "barbarians" (East Goths) who were Arians (Christians who denied the divinity of Christ), while Boethius was a Catholic.

Boethius was the single most educated and intelligent man in a dying civilization. His life's goal was to translate all of Plato and Aristotle from Greek into Latin (because the number of people who knew Greek was decreasing) and to reconcile them philosophically. He finished only Aristotle's logical works (which was all that the next seven centuries knew of Aristotle), a book of philosophical theology on the Trinity, and his shorter and more popular little masterpiece, *The Consolation of Philosophy,* which was one of the four most popular books in what was left of Western civilization for the next 1000 years, together with the Bible and Augustine's *Confessions* and *The City of God*.

Philosophers often write short, simple books as well as long, difficult ones, and (surprise, surprise!) the former turn out to be beloved masterpieces.

Theodoric employed Boethius as a consul, and sent him on diplomatic peace missions to the Eastern (Byzantine) Emperor Justin I. But he came to suspect Boethius of treason (probably because Boethius was more concerned with union than with the rights of the West against the East), and had him imprisoned, tortured, and executed. His little masterpiece, *The Consolation of Philosophy,* was written in prison while awaiting execution.

Like many medieval philosophers, Boethius attempted to synthesize Plato and Aristotle, the two greatest philosophical minds of his time. At the heart of Boethius' synthesis is his treatment of "the problem of universals," the issue that most separated these two philosophers. This is found in his commentary on a commentary on Aristotle's logic, the *Isagoge* by Porphyry, which asks three questions:

(1) Are universals ("genera and species") objective realities or mere ideas in the mind?

(2) If objective, are they corporeal (material, bodily entities) or incorporeal?

(3) If incorporeal, do they exist apart from sensible things or only in them? (This third question is the one that most basically separates Plato and Aristotle.)

Boethius's answer is Yes to all three, but with the qualification that their existence apart from sensible things is only in minds, first of all God's mind and secondly ours. So his solution here is closer to Aristotle than to Plato.

But *The Consolation of Philosophy* is more Platonic than Aristotelian. Aristotle wins the purely intellectual, scholarly contest, but Plato wins the existential human contest of consoling a man in the face of death.

*Consolation* was written in prison by a man waiting to die, and thus naturally compares with Socrates' *Apology*, *Crito*, and *Phaedo*. It is the prisoner's reflection on the meaning of life and death, good and evil, happiness and misery, God and man, fate and freedom. It is highly "existential" (personal) yet highly rational—a combination much more typical of premodern philosophers than modern.

Boethius, unlike Augustine, clearly distinguishes what can be known by philosophical reason alone from what is known only by faith in divine revelation; and since it is the consolation of *Philosophy* rather than of religion, he confines himself to what can be known about these great questions by philosophical reason alone without religious faith or appeal to divine revelation. In fact, Boethius is the first to practice a clear distinction between what can be known by each of these two enterprises. Boethius straddles two eras: he was the last classical (Roman) philosopher, who knew the whole of both Plato and Aristotle, and the first medieval ("scholastic") philosopher (sharp distinguisher of reason from faith).

*Consolation* is a synthesis of themes from Socrates, Plato, Aristotle, and the Stoics; and it passed these themes, like a baton in a relay race, to the next great era in history, the Middle Ages. It also passed down the essential structure of university education for the next 1000+ years in the "seven liberal arts"—the "quadrivium" of arithmetic, geometry, astronomy (or physics), and music, and the "trivium" of grammar (language), dialectic (logic), and rhetoric (effective use of language and logic for persuasion), which was first formulated by Plato in Book 7 of the *Republic*.

*Consolation* is a blend of prose and poetry (half its chapters are poems), and of monolog and Socratic dialog. The part of Socrates is played by the allegorical figure Lady Philosophy, who ministers rational "consolation" to the condemned Boethius in careful stages, rising from obvious common sense through the surprises of philosophy to a solution to the classic puzzle of reconciling divine omniscience and human free will (both of which Boethius believes can be demonstrated by rational philosophy).

*Consolation* is one of the most popular and readable books of philosophy ever written. It is a synthesis of ancient wisdom, and therefore strikes the typically modern reader as excitingly exotic and unusual (for in an age of radical anti-traditionalism, tradition appears the most radical option of all). Its three main philosophical issues are:

(1) The content of happiness, the "summum bonum," both theoretically (what is it? money? fame? honor? health? pleasure? power? virtue? contemplation?) and practically (how can we attain it?).

(2) The problem of evil: in a world created and controlled by a good, just, wise, and all-powerful God, how can the righteous man suffer evils that are deserved by the wicked?—which seems to be exactly what is happening to Boethius. It is a philosophical version of the Book of *Job*.

(3) The problem of reconciling divine providence, predestination, foreknowledge, or fate with human free will and free choice.

Rather than summarizing each step of the argument of *Consolation*, or summarizing Boethius's essential answer to each of these three questions, I thought it would intrigue the reader more if I presented some typical passages from the book itself as "appetizers." You will recognize many Socratic and Stoic influences.

**(1) He who is burdened by fears and desires is not master of himself . . . he fastens the** chain by which he will be drawn.

**(2) If there is a God, why is there evil? And if there is no God, how can there be** good? (quoted from Lactantius, who quoted it from Epicurus).

**(3) Adverse fortune is more beneficial to men than prosperous fortune . . . [for] good fortune deceives, adverse fortune teaches. . . . No man can ever be secure until he has been forsaken by Fortune.**

**(4) Nothing is miserable unless you think it so; and on the other hand, nothing** brings happiness unless you are content with it.

**(5) The sound of a voice can be given equally to many hearers, but money cannot be distributed among many persons without impoverishing those who give it up.**

**(6) Do you try to satisfy your desires with external goods which are foreign to you because you have no good within you which belongs to you? What an upside-down state of affairs when a man who is divine by his gift of reason thinks his excellence depends on the possession of lifeless bric-a-brac!**

**(7) You choose to call things by false names . . . material possessions are not rightly called riches, worldly power is not true power, and public honor is not true honor.**

**(8) The universe carries out its changing process in concord and with stable faith (fidelity) . . . the conflicting seeds of things are held by everlasting law . . . all this harmonious order of things is achieved by love, which rules the earth and the seas and commands the heavens. But if love should slack the reins, all that is now joined in mutual love would wage continual war. . . . O how happy the human race would be if that love which rules the heavens ruled also your souls!**

**(9) (to God:) You rule the immense heavens, rule also the earth in stable concord.**

(10) Mortal men laboriously pursue different interests along many different paths, but all strive to reach the same goal of happiness . . . perfect happiness is the perfect state in which all goods are possessed . . . there is naturally implanted in the minds of men the desire for the true good, even though foolish error draws them toward false goods . . . like the drunk who cannot find his way home.

(11) Nature guides the reins of all things: lions . . . shake off their chains; . . . the chattering bird in a narrow cage . . . can escape; . . . a treetop bent down by heavy pressure . . . looks back to heaven again; . . . all things seek again their proper courses and rejoice when they return to them.

(12) If they [bodily pleasures] can produce happiness (not just contentment but blessedness), then there is no reason why beasts should not be called happy. . . . For you are not bigger than an elephant, nor stronger than a bull, nor as quick as a tiger.

(13) You do not look for gold in the green trees . . . you do not set your nets in the high mountains when you want a fish . . . but when it comes to the location of the good which you desire, you dig the earth in search of the good which soars above the star-filled heavens.

(14) If something is found to be imperfect in its kind, there must necessarily be something of that same kind which is perfect. For without a standard of perfection we cannot judge anything to be imperfect.

(15) Nothing can be conceived of as better than God.

(16) Everything naturally desires to continue in existence and to avoid harm.

(17) The good are always powerful and the evil always weak and futile . . . vice never goes unpunished nor virtue unrewarded . . . the good prosper and the evil suffer.

(18) Since both seek the good, but good men obtain it and evil men do not, it follows that good men have power but evil men are impotent.

(19) Just as virtue itself is the reward of virtuous men, so wickedness itself is the punishment of the wicked.

(20) Just as virtue can raise a person above human nature, so vice lowers those whom it has seduced from the condition of men . . . one who abandons virtue ceases to be a man, since he cannot share in the divine nature, and instead becomes a beast.

**(21)** The wicked are happier when they are punished than when they evade justice . . . when they seem to escape chastisement they are in reality undergoing more-severe punishment.

**(22)** "When I consider your argument, I find that nothing could be more true. But if we consider the ordinary judgment of men, who is likely to find these ideas credible?" "That is true," Philosophy answered, "because men cannot raise eyes accustomed to darkness to the light of clear truth. They are like those birds who can see at night but are blind in the daylight. For as long as they fix their attention on their own feelings rather than on the true nature of things, they think that the license of passion and immunity from punishment bring happiness."

**(23)** Those who injure others are more unhappy than those whom they injure.

**(24)** Criminals ought to be brought to justice as sick men are taken to the doctor, so that their disease of guilt might be cured by punishment. In this way, defense attorneys . . . would become accusers.

**(25)** There is no such thing as chance.

**(26)** (If there is no free will, then) **the structure of all human affairs must collapse. For it is pointless to assign rewards and punishments . . . vice and virtue will be without meaning . . . and the Author of all good must be made responsible for all human vice . . . what is the point in hope or prayer when everything that man desires is determined by unalterable process?**

**(27)** Whatever is known is known according to the nature of the knower.

**(28)** Eternity is the whole, perfect, and simultaneous possession of endless life.

**(29)** He [God] sees all things in His eternal present as you see some things in your temporal present . . . divine foreknowledge does not change the natures and properties of things, it simply sees things present before it as they will later turn out to be in what we regard as the future.

# 38. Pseudo-Dionysius the Areopagite (ca. 500)

Of the 100 most important philosophers, his is the name you would probably choose (and guess) the last. He was actually an early sixth-century Christian monk and mystic in Syria who pretended to be the first-century disciple of St. Paul mentioned in the New Testament (Acts 17:34), Dionysius of the Areopagus (Mars Hill) in Athens. It was a literary device common in ancient times—e.g., the later author of *Ecclesiastes* calls himself ancient King Solomon. But the Middle Ages, lacking scientific historical expertise, took him literally and ascribed to him great authority because of his apparent closeness to St. Paul. St. Thomas Aquinas quotes him no less than 1700 times.

Even if this was a "pious fraud," as a cynical historian would say, it providentially exercised a good and necessary corrective to the rationalism that was a danger inherent in the logical methods of "scholastic" (school) philosophies of the West, especially after the Great Schism of 1054 built a spiritual wall of suspicion between East and West for centuries, during which Dionysius was the only Eastern writer still revered and used in the West. Examples of Western "rationalism" (over-estimation of reason's power) are Boethius's attempt to logically demonstrate the Trinity and Anselm's attempt to demonstrate both the Trinity and the necessity of the Incarnation by reason alone.

Dionysius's most important book is *On the Divine Names*. Its essential points are:

1. God alone knows Himself, therefore He alone can reveal Himself, as He did in scripture. We must begin with our data: scripture's names for God.

2. But even divinely revealed names cannot tell us the nature or essence of God because these names must be borrowed from finite creatures, which are the only beings our finite minds can comprehend. We cannot know God directly, therefore we cannot name Him directly.

3. Naming Him indirectly, from creatures, involves three steps or stages:

A. "Affirmative theology" affirms all the names that God has revealed to us: God is being, good, one, just, loving, wise, omnipotent, etc. We accept our *data*. This is as true for the philosophical theologian as for the uneducated believer.

B. But if we are wise, we cannot interpret this data, these names, literally and univocally, i.e., as having one and the same meaning when we predicate them of God and of creatures. E.g., God cannot be just as man is just, for human justice is a set of reciprocal relationships between finite beings that are relative to each other. It is based on what is owed. But God is not relative to creatures, and owes nothing. To take another example, "Truth" for us means the correspondence of our minds to objective reality which measures them, but nothing can measure God's mind. And "Good" for us means "serving an end," but God is not a means to an end, or even Himself *an* end, but *the* end of everything.

Thus "negative theology" must deny that God is anything humanly conceivable. As Augustine often said, "if you comprehend it, it is not God."

This corrective to rationalism would become an essential feature of theological orthodoxy even in the West. Aquinas would later say, "this is the supreme knowledge of God: to know that He is unknowable." We can "apprehend" Him but not "comprehend" Him. All we can know univocally (literally) about God, Aquinas taught, is what God is *not*. Positive statements about Him are not univocal but analogical; they tell us not what He *is* but what He is *like*. Even this is wrong, for God is like nothing, but some things are more like Him than others (persons more than things, good more than evil).

C. But denying that He is truth, light, goodness, being, etc. does not mean He is falsehood, darkness, evil, or nonbeing. So, in the third step, "superlative theology," we must correct our corrections, and say that God is "super-being," "super-good," etc. He infinitely surpasses all that we can say or think of Him, positive or negative.

This is not irrationalism. It is not a vague feeling. It is a clear, three-step rational insight. It says something definite.

Dionysius also left us two other books, *On the Celestial Hierarchy* and *On the Ecclesiastical Hierarchy*, in which he further specified the popular Western idea of natural "order" (*ordo,* one of the essential meanings of *logos*) as *hierarchical*.

What this means is that all creatures stream or flow from God in descending ranks and return to Him by retracing these steps. This is true of all created things: angels, men, the Church, and nature. Dionysius popularized the *exitus-redditus* (emanation and return) cosmology of Plotinus (ch. 33) to the West, where it would become a constituent part of the medieval world-view.

As a Neoplatonist, Dionysius calls this cascade of beings an "illumination." This term does not mean a gift of light to already existing beings (as it does, e.g., in Augustine) but the gift of light or intelligibility which *is* the essence of being. The creation is really a manifestation, a theophany, a "light-giving." It is more like a fireworks display than a speech or a newspaper.

Man's essential task, given this cosmic hierarchy, is to "return" to God, his ultimate Source and End. And the essential fuel for this journey is love. It is the divine love for us that radiated all beings, including man, into existence; and it is man's love for God that draws man out of himself and back to God—even "into" God, for man's ultimate end is *theosis,* divinization, sharing the divine nature (II Peter 1:4).

Thus Dionysius calls love an "ecstasy" (literally, a "standing-outside-yourself"). Love transforms the mystically self-forgetful lover into the object of his love, whether that object is human or divine. To love x is to participate in x. As in Augustine, love is gravity, as in Dante gravity is love, "the love that moves the sun and all the starts."

# 39. John Scotus Erigena (815–877)

### His Life and Times

The "Dark Ages" came roughly (and when they came, they did come roughly) between 500 and 1000 A.D. The most remarkable thinker during this period was John Scotus Erigena. He was one of the Irishmen who helped save Western civilization. (See *How the Irish Saved Civilization* by Thomas Cahill.) He was called "Scotus" ("the Scot") since the Irish were then called Scots.

"All that is positively known of him, apart from his writings, is that he spent some years in France at the court of Charles the Bald, with whom he seems to have been on terms of familiar friendship. The story is told that one day, seated at table with him, the king asked, 'What divides a sot from a Scot?' To which Erigena blandly replied; 'Only the table.'" (Gerald Bullett, *The English Mystics,* p. 44.) The pun works in Latin too: "Quid distat inter sottum et Scottum?"

According to some (non-Anglophile) sources, he was stabbed to death by his English students. (People cared more about philosophy then than now.)

### His Historical Significance

Etienne Gilson says that his philosophy "offered to the Latins the possibility, one might almost say the temptation, of entering once and for all the way initiated by the Greek theologians, [especially] Denis the Areopagite (ch. 38). . . . Had this invitation been accepted, a neoplatonic philosophy would no doubt have prevailed in Western Europe up to the end of the middle ages. The fact that Erigena's example was not followed is, on the contrary, a sure sign that what we today call Europe was already groping its way toward a different type of metaphysical speculation." (*History of Christian Philosophy in the Middle Ages.*)

The essential difference between East and West, Greeks and Latins, Erigena and Aquinas, Neoplatonists and Aristotelians, is in metaphysics. For the Aristotelians, *Being* is the absolute, God is Being, and creatures are beings. Creation is the gift of being to beings by God, whose primary name is Being ("I AM"). For the Neoplatonists, Oneness is the absolute, and is "above being." (See ch. 33, Plotinus.) Being is merely finitude and plurality. Erigena defines being as **"whatever can be perceived by the senses or understood by the intellect."** It follows that God is not Being (for He cannot be perceived or defined); God is The One, creatures are the many, and creation is the procession or descent of the many from The One, just as in Plotinus.

Augustine too knew and loved Neoplatonic philosophers, but while Erigena Neoplatonized Christianity, Augustine Christianized Neoplatonism. (See Aquinas's summary of Augustine on page 29.)

### Faith and Reason

All medieval philosophers sought some kind of synthesis or marriage of Christian faith and philosophical reason, though in different ways—some intimate, some distant. Erigena distinguishes faith and reason, and prioritizes faith over reason, but *identifies* religion and philosophy as the same thing. He writes, **"No one can enter heaven except by philosophy."**

He allegorizes the Gospel passage in which Peter and John run to Jesus's empty tomb on Easter morning. Younger John outruns Peter but lets Peter enter the tomb first. The tomb = divine revelation (Scripture), Peter = faith, and John = reason. The point is that when reason lets faith lead, it will receive illumination. Christian philosophy is "faith seeking understanding" (*fides quaerens intellectum*), as Anselm would later formulate this relationship. Faith is the precondition for understanding the ultimate meaning of everything, for god is the ultimate meaning of everything, and faith is the precondition for understanding God.

### "The Division of Nature"

Erigena's masterpiece, *The Division of Nature,* is a vast reinterpretation of Christian theology by Neoplatonic dialectic.

**"Dialectic"** for Erigena means not "the art of logical argument" but the process by which both concepts *and* realities come to be what they are. There are two phases to this process: **"division,"** by which The One produces the many, and **"analysis,"** by which the many return to The One. The process is simultaneously cosmological and logical. Like Hegel (ch. 70), Erigena identifies the laws of reality with the laws of thought. As thought divides and recombines concepts—e.g., it divides "substance" down into "material" and "spiritual," "material substances" into "living (organisms) and nonliving," and "organisms" into "plants" and "animals," and then "analyzes" or classifies plants and animals up into organisms, organisms and minerals into material substances, and material and spiritual things into substances—so reality proceeds in the same way. "God created the universe" means, for Erigena, not "The primary, eternal Being gave being to temporal beings" but "The One produced the many by division." The formula sounds pantheistic, as if God divided Himself, and that creatures are merely parts of God; but Erigena clearly did not mean that.

"Nature" means for Erigena everything that can be or even not be. It is the broadest possible term, broader than "being." He divides Nature into four kinds:

(1) **Nature which creates and is not created.** This is God as the transcendent Creator, the One, the absolutely First.

(2) **Nature which is created and also creates.** This is the Divine Ideas, immaterial Platonic Forms in the Mind of God, the Logos, the Second Person of the Trinity. These Ideas are eternally conceived by the Divine Mind and are the universal models, archetypes, exemplars, or ideals which contain all possible particular examples of them. In this sense they "create" (divide into) more particular ideas (by "division") and finally, concrete individual material things. (Matter is maximally dispersed, maximally many, maximally far from The One.)

(3) **Nature which is created and does not create**. This is the material universe.

(4) **Nature which does not create and is not created**. This is God conceived as the final end of all things.

These four parts are really only two, God (1 and 4) and two kinds of creatures, immaterial and material (2 and 3). God can be thought of as the Beginning (1) or the End (4) of all things, and creatures can be looked at as in their Divine Ideas (2) or as the concrete individuals (3) that flow from, but are all logically contained or implied in, their universal Ideas.

To us this sounds like a radically foreign language, a strangely abstract and immaterial way of looking at things, an attempt at a God's-eye point of view. That psychological fact shows the truth of Gilson's historical point in the third paragraph of this chapter.

## God

Since being is "perceived or conceived," and since God therefore is not being, God is unknowable, *even to Himself* (this claim was later labeled heretical by the Church) until He "descends" into manyness. To put the point in another, parallel way, God is infinite, and the Infinite cannot be circumscribed or defined, and only what can be defined can be known, therefore God cannot be known. (Do you see any one of those three premises as questionable?)

Erigena's concern is to safeguard God's absolute transcendence over all things. (This is the extreme opposite of pantheism, although some of his statements are easily misunderstood as pantheism.) Like "the Buddha-mind" or "Only-mind" in Zen Buddhism, God is "no-thing." The question "What is God?" is meaningless and unanswerable because God is not a "what": He is neither a concrete individual nor an abstract Platonic universal, an Idea, since both of these are finite and plural (one of many).

How then can we say anything meaningful about God? Erigena repeats the answer of Pseudo-Dionysius the Areopagite (ch. 38): we must do three things:

(1) "Affirmative theology" affirms all the divine names God revealed to us in Scripture, e.g., "God is good" or "God is being."

(2) "Negative theology" denies that any of these names defines, confines, or categorizes the infinite One. God is *not* literally good, or being.

(3) "Superlative theology" explains that the reason for these negations is not that God is less but more than any of these names. He is not good but "super-good" (more than good) and "super-being."

Charles Williams draws the practical conclusion from this theology: that of every-thing in the universe we must pray twice and say both "This too is Thou" and "Neither is this Thou." On the one hand, everything is a manifestation of God. The whole universe is a second scripture, a book of created signs all of which manifest something of the Cre-ator. (Christianity is not deism.) On the other hand, God is infinitely more, removed, and above all things. (Christianity is not pantheism or paganism.)

## The Divine Ideas

All medieval philosophers, unless they were Nominalists, who denied any reality to uni-versals, believed in Platonic Ideas in the Mind of God, where Augustine had located them. This produced a theological problem, for this seems to make them neither creatures (for they are temporal, while the Ideas are eternal) nor the Creator (for He is one, while the Ideas are many).

Augustine and Aquinas both identify the many Ideas with the one God Himself as knowable and imitable by many possible creatures. Some of the Eastern theologians called them "divine energies," and saw them as something like beams of sunlight eter-nally streaming from the sun (or the Son). In one sense they are divine, in another sense they are creatures. Erigena calls them "co-eternal but not quite co-eternal" with God. This sounds like a compromise or a confusion, but it means that they are eternally "made" (caused) by God in His Mind (Word, Logos, Son). They are not the Creator but creatures, for they are finite and plural, while God is infinite and one.

## Erigena's Limitations

What makes this idea difficult to understand is that Erigena sees producing, or making, or creating, not primarily as a relationship of efficient causality but of formal causality. The Aristotelian distinction among the "four causes" may help you to sort out just what Erigena is saying here. He is reducing efficient to formal causality, or identifying efficient with formal causality, or speaking the language of formal rather than efficient causality. An efficient cause accounts for the existence of its effect; a formal cause accounts for the intelligibility or intelligible essence of its effect. The effect of an efficient cause is a substance (a thing-that-exists); the effect of a formal cause is a form.

Another way to put this point is that Erigena does *not* say that the eternal creation of the universal Ideas (forms) in the Mind of God is followed by another creation, the cre-ation in time of individual things (substances, beings, things-that-exist). Formal causality alone is enough. For him all beings are already formally contained in their Ideas, since these Ideas are their (formal) causes.

Here is a third way to put the point: Erigena does not clearly distinguish efficient causality from formal causality, or existence from essences (forms); therefore, he does not distinguish an explanation of the existence of an individual substance from an explanation of its universal form, essence, or Idea. Once again we see how alien this Neoplatonic way of thinking has become to our Aristotelian or Thomistic minds.

Another indication of this confusion is Erigena's view that the Fall into sin was also a fall into materiality and multiplicity. If we had not sinned, he says, we would not be divided into two sexes. (This thesis was also condemned as a heresy.) The consequence of the Fall was not merely evil but also multiplicity, in the universe as well as in man. (For Erigena sees the whole universe as something "in" human knowledge; thus when man fell, the whole universe fell with him.) Like Plotinus, he almost (but not quite) identifies evil with multiplicity and matter, almost identifies the Fall with what we would call the Creation.

Like most medieval philosophers, Erigena's intention was not to change, but to understand, the meaning of scriptural revelation. But his Neoplatonic means proved only partly and not wholly fitting for that end. Of course, this must be true of *all* philosophical interpretations—no philosophy is perfect, either theologically or even philosophically—but some can be less imperfect than others.

# 40. St. Anselm (1034–1109)

St. Anselm was the abbot of a Benedictine monastery in England in the eleventh century, when Europe was gradually awakening from the Dark Ages and constructing a Christian civilization and culture, largely through the educational efforts of the monasteries.

A few days before he died, one of his fellow monks told him that he would probably die in a few days. He replied, "If it is His will, I shall gladly obey, but if He should prefer me to stay with you just long enough to solve the question of the origin of the soul, which I have kept turning over in my mind, I would gratefully accept the chance, for I doubt whether anybody else will solve it when I am gone." His prophecy was correct.

Anselm is perhaps history's greatest admirer and disciple of Augustine, both in style (which, like Augustine's, is both poetically beautiful and brilliantly intellectual) and in content (a Christian Platonism, or Platonic Christianity). His main divergence from Augustine is his great faith in logic's ability to prove all the essential mysteries of Christianity, even the Trinity and the Incarnation, by "necessary reasons," at least in theory. His *Cur Deus Homo* ("Why God Became Man") attempts to deduce the rational necessity of the Incarnation. (Aquinas would soften this claim to "the *fittingness* of the Incarnation.")

Yet in practice, for Anselm, all depends on a faith beginning. And this aspect is authentically Augustinian. He famously says **I do not seek to understand in order that I may believe, but I believe in order that I may understand. For I also believe this: that unless I believe, I shall not understand.** This is not just clever rhetoric or empty piety but an implicit a fortiori argument from analogy: Without personal faith and trust, we cannot really understand each other; why should this not apply even more to our understanding of God?

To put the previous two points together, for Anselm the whole building of rational philosophy depends on faith as its foundation; yet the building is constructed entirely of reason and reaches high into the heavens (including the Trinity and the Incarnation).

Anselm is eminently worth reading for his own sake. especially his very short, very "packed" summary of Christian theology in his *Proslogion*; but he is famous among philosophers mainly for a single argument for the existence of God, which Kant christened "the ontological argument."

No argument about anything has ever generated more response from other philosophers, or more controversy. There are important philosophers who accept it (Bonaventura, Scotus, Descartes, Spinoza, Leibnitz, Hegel, Plantinga), and important theistic philosophers who reject it (Aquinas, Pascal, Locke, Kant, Kierkegaard, Adler), and some who find it brilliant and successful but not a proof (Barth, Gilson).

Perhaps justice is done to Anselm's argument only if we see it as an ultimate *explanation* rather than a *proof.* (The word "demonstration" can mean either.) By "defining" God (negatively) as "that than which nothing greater can be conceived" and by distinguishing God from creatures by saying that God exists necessarily, by His essence, while creatures exist contingently, from their causes, Anselm explains, justifies and shows the intelligibility of *everything*. Creatures' essence is not existence, thus they need causes. God's essence is existence, thus He needs no cause or explanation other than His own essential nature. The universe exists because God created it; God exists because God is God. So if God exists, everything is intelligible; if not, nothing is.

Here, in Anselm's own words from his *Proslogion*, is the most famous argument in the history of human thought. Note its very Augustinian "bookends" or context, both before and after the argument itself (points I and IV below): this is the most important part of it for Anselm, but it is almost always omitted in philosophy anthologies.

(I) The religious context:

**I do not seek to understand so that I may believe, but I believe so that I may understand. For I believe this also, that "unless I believe, I shall not understand" (Isaiah 7:9). So then, Lord, You who give understanding to faith, grant me that I may understand, as much as You see fit, that You exist as we believe You to exist, and that You are what we believe You to be.**

(II) The argument:

(1) **Now we believe that You are something-than-which-nothing-greater-can-be-thought.**

(2) **Or can it be that a thing of such a nature does not exist, since "the fool has said in his heart that there is no God" (Psalm 13:1; 52:1)?**

(3) **But surely when this same fool hears what I am speaking about, namely "something-than-which-nothing-greater-can-be-thought," he understands what he hears, and what he understands is in his mind, even if he does not understand that it actually exists.**

(4) **For it is one thing for an object to exist in the mind, and another thing to understand [judge] that an object actually exists. Thus, when a painter plans beforehand what he is going to execute, he has it (the picture) in his mind, but he does not yet think [judge] that it actually exists because he has not yet executed it. However when he has actually painted it, then he both has it in his mind and understands [judges] that it exists because he has now made it.**

(5) **Even the fool, then, is forced to agree that something-than-which-nothing-greater-can-be-thought exists in the mind, since he understands this when he hears it, and whatever is understood exists in the mind.**

(6) (a) **And surely that-than-which-a greater-cannot-be-thought cannot exist in the mind alone.**

    (b) **For if it exists solely in the mind, it can be *thought* to exist in reality also,**

    (c) **which is greater.**

(d) **If, then, that-than-which-a greater-cannot-be-thought exists in the mind alone, then this same that-than-which-a greater-*cannot*-be-thought is that-than-which-a-greater-*can*-be-thought.**

(e) **But this is obviously impossible.**

(f) **Therefore there is absolutely no doubt that something-than-which-a-greater-cannot-be-thought exists both in the mind and in reality.**

(III) The metaphysical point of the argument: the distinction between necessary being (whose essence is existence) and contingent being (whose essence is not existence):

**And surely this being so truly exists that it cannot be even thought not to exist. For something can be thought to exist that cannot be thought not to exist, and this is greater than that which can be thought not to exist. And You, Lord our God, are this being.**

**In fact, everything else there is, except you alone, can be thought of as not existing.**

(IV) The existential point of the argument: since there is one objectively real God Who contains all perfections, there is one subjectively real human happiness, which consists in the love of this God:

**"One thing is necessary" (Luke 10:42). This is that one thing necessary in which is every good. . . . Why then do you wander about so much, O little man, seeking the goods of your soul and body? Love the one good in which all good things are, and that is sufficient. . . . For what do you love, O my flesh? What do you desire, O my soul? There, there is whatever you love, whatever you desire . . .**

**And surely if someone else who you loved in every way as you love yourself possessed that same blessedness, your joy would be doubled, for you would rejoice as much for him as for yourself. . . . Indeed, to the degree that each one loves another, he will rejoice in the good of that other; therefore, just as each one in that perfect happiness will love God incomparably more than himself and all others with him, so he will rejoice immeasurably more over the happiness of God than over his own happiness and that of all the others with him. But if they love God with their whole heart, their whole mind, their whole soul, while yet their whole heart and mind and soul is not equal to the greatness of this love, then assuredly they will so rejoice with their whole heart and mind and soul that their whole heart and mind and soul will not be equal to the fullness of their joy. . . . The whole of that joy, then, will not enter into those who rejoice, but those who rejoice will enter wholly into that joy . . . which 'eye has not seen, nor ear heard, nor has it entered into the heart of man' (I Cor. 2:9)."**

# 41. Peter Abelard (1079–1142)

## His Life

His name was really Pierre (Peter) le Pallet; "Abelard" was an adopted surname. He was the most brilliant philosopher of his time. He was such a popular teacher, leading his students rationally step by step, that they followed him wherever he went also step by step, from one city or school to another. His *Sic et Non* ("Yes or No") put hundreds of opposing quotations from the Church Fathers into dialectical argument and then reconciled them. This was an early version of the later Scholastic method used by Aquinas (ch. 50). Peter the Venerable called him "the Socrates of the Gauls (French), the Plato of the West, our Aristotle."

Philosophy meant largely logic at the time; for except for Aristotle's logical works, none of the writings of Plato or Aristotle had been rediscovered yet in the West. Abelard was not only logically brilliant but also personally impatient: he quarreled with all his teachers, both the extreme Nominalist Roscelin and the extreme Platonic realist William of Champeaux. Defeating both in debate, he wrote, "I began to think of myself as the only philosopher in the world."

He could not, however, defeat St. Bernard of Clairvaux, who did not debate him in philosophy but called him an arrogant rationalist and a heretic and persuaded the Pope to condemn some of his theses, especially in ethics (see below).

The drama of Abelard and Eloise is one of the most fascinating love stories in history. Abelard became private tutor to 16-year-old Eloise, niece of Fulbert, canon of the cathedral of Notre Dame. Eloise was both beautiful and brilliant. She mastered Greek, Latin, and Hebrew, philosophy, theology, and classics. They became secret lovers, and she became pregnant. Abelard, who was not yet a cleric, proposed secret marriage to her; but she refused, writing that she would rather be his whore than his wife, since marriage would betray the ideal of what a true philosopher ought to be: a cleric married to his work. (They had a significantly higher concept of philosophy and a lower one of marriage than we do today!) He agreed, for the sake of his career. (Would Romeo do that?) But they could not hide the relationship, and revengeful Uncle Fulda sent men to castrate Abelard. (**They removed from me those parts in which I had offended**, he wrote in *The History of My Calamities*.) Eloise joined a convent and Abelard a monastery, from which their love was expressed only by passionate and eloquent letters. Their son Astrolabe, who was raised by Abelard's sister, was named after a measuring instrument in astronomy. (Philosophers are usually very weird when it comes to children.)

## Faith and Reason

Abelard was certainly not a rationalist in any modern sense. He neither ranked reason above faith nor separated the two. He wrote, in response to charges of heresy, **I do not want to be a philosopher if it is necessary to deny Paul; I do not want to be Aristotle if it is necessary to be separated from Christ.** But he did nearly identify the Faith with reason, subjecting everything to purely rational scrutiny. Bernard said that to him, "all was clear, even mystery."

He tightened up the concept of reason itself, emphasizing not contemplation (the "first act of the mind") but proof (the "third act of the mind"), an orderly, logical demonstration worthy to be called scientific, rather like a modern mathematical logician or "analytic philosopher."

## The Problem of Universals

His earlier teacher, Roscelin, had taught that a universal was nothing but a "flatus vocis," a sound, literally a "fart of the voice." It was not even a confused concept. Roscelin was later accused (but not convicted) of heresy for applying his Nominalism to the doctrine of the Trinity; for if only individuals are real, there can be no common divine nature shared by the three Persons, so that they are three gods rather than one God.

The doctrine of Original Sin is also difficult to believe in if one is a Nominalist, for if there is no such thing as universal human nature, how can it have been affected and wounded by the first actual sin of the first humans? Abelard, who was closer to Nominalism than to Realism, answered that each of us creates our own individual "original sin." We do not come into the world morally wounded and weakened in our nature because there is no universal "human nature."

His later teacher, William of Champeaux, taught, like Plato, that universals were substances common to many individuals. Abelard's logical critiques forced William to modify his position and say that what was common to many individuals of a species was not a substance but a "non-differentness" among them.

Abelard's position was definitely a modified Nominalism. He said that a universal is not any kind of real entity but merely a grammatical or logical entity, a class of words *(nomina)*, or rather a logical function of words. They have meaning because they signify individuals, not natures (essences). Abelard writes, **"We appeal to no essence."** The objective ground of common terms is not any common reality but only the fact that individuals *resemble* each other. They designate *confused images* of these similar individuals.

The "bottom line" is that universal terms signify nothing more than individual terms signify. There is no more in "man" or "humanity" than in "Socrates." So universality is not a problem of metaphysics at all, since universals have no kind of reality. It is merely a problem of semantics, of the meaning of words. (This is a typically modern position.)

## Ethics

Abelard's ethical philosophy is found in his *Scito Teipsum* ("Know Thyself"). His distinctive point is that the moral or ethical good consists exclusively in an individual's intention, not in the act itself, its object, its end, or its circumstances. This would be the position, later, of Kant, the most influential ethical philosopher of modern times. **An action is good not because it contains within it some good but because it issues from a good intention.** The same is true for evil. The morality of an act is identical to, and not more than, the morality of the intention. A good act adds nothing to a good intention.

Augustine, earlier, and Aquinas, later, would list *three* "moral determinants" rather than just one. For them, although intention was the most important, because the most personal and interior, the objective nature of the act and the objective situation or circumstances also had to be relevant and to count in making the act morally good or bad. There was a natural connection between the subjective intention and the objective act. One does not give up his life for another out of hate, nor does one rape out of love.

There is a close logical connection between Abelard's metaphysical Nominalism and his moral subjectivism or individualism, since intention is always an individual's intention, while the nature of a human act (and also its object, its end, and even its circumstances) is something common or universal. If there are no essences, no universal natures, then a human act cannot be judged as right or wrong because it is an act of this or that nature. If this is true, then there is no objective moral order. There are no "natural" or "unnatural" acts. We cannot violate human nature if it does not exist. (This is a typically modern position, not a typically ancient or medieval one, in both its Nominalism and its subjectivism.)

There is also an obvious *psychological* connection between Abelard's philosophy and his life, between his theory and his practice, between his philosophical separation of the intention from the act and his personal desire to justify his objectively-sinful sexual practice by subjectively-good personal intentions. Abelard is a very up-to-date thinker.

## Selected Bibliography:

*Heloise and Abelard* by Etienne Gilson,
*Peter Abelard* (novel) by Helen Waddell

# 42. St. Bonaventure (c. 1225–1274)

## His Life and Times

St. Bonaventure was a Franciscan contemporary and personal friend of the Dominican St. Thomas Aquinas. They both lived during the middle of the thirteenth century. They both taught at the University of Paris. And they both were canonized as saints and Doctors (Teachers) of the Church.

*Thirteenth, Greatest of Centuries* is the surprising but defensible title of a book by a great medievalist (Walsh). Philosophically, the thirteenth century was a time of great challenge, for the major works of Aristotle had just been rediscovered and translated into Latin. (Before that, the West had only his logic.) The medievals had nicknames for all the great philosophers—Aquinas was "the Angelic Doctor," Bonaventure was "the Seraphic Doctor," Duns Scotus, a century later, was "the Subtle Doctor"—but Aristotle was simply "*The* Philosopher." But this greatest of philosophers, regarded by many as the supreme achievement of human reason, contradicted at least three major Christian dogmas: that the world was created rather than eternal; that God providentially knew, loved, and cared for the world; and that the individual human soul was immortal.

Three responses developed to this challenge.

(1) Radical "Latin Averroists" followed the Arabian Muslim philosopher Averroes (ch. 48) in putting Aristotle in first place and religious dogmas second. They negotiated his contradictions to Christianity by teaching something like a theory of "double truth" (this term is associated with Siger of Brabant): that a proposition could be true theologically but false philosophically, or vice versa; that truth for philosophers was so different from truth for ordinary believers that there could be real contradictions between the two.

Averroes had confronted the same faith-vs.-reason problem a few centuries before. (Muslim civilization was centuries ahead of Christian in the "Dark Ages" (sixth through tenth centuries), and their philosophers had known Aristotle much earlier than the Christian philosophers of Europe.) The Qur'an, like the Bible, clearly teaches creation, providence, and the soul's immortality and eternal judgment. Averroes' answer to this dilemma was to interpret divine revelation as an inferior, symbolic, or anthropomorphic version of the ultimate, literal truth which was found only in Aristotle.

Later, in the West, revisionist" or "liberal" or "modernist" Christian theologians of the nineteenth and twentieth centuries did the same thing regarding the contradiction between the supernaturalism of Biblical miracles and the naturalism of modern science. (Actually, naturalism is not science but philosophy: it is an "ism.")

(2) Traditionalist Augustinians like Bonaventure returned to Augustine and his

Platonism and demoted Aristotle to second place at best: although Aristotle may be the master of natural science, Plato was the master of metaphysical wisdom. As in the famous painting "The School of Athens," Aristotle points to the earth, Plato points up to the heavens. That is why, for Bonaventure, Augustine was wise to prefer Plato to Aristotle. Bonaventure knew Aristotle very well, but when he used Aristotelian terminology it was to make the Augustinian points, as we shall see below.

(3) Neither "radical progressive" nor "traditionalist conservative" in philosophy, Thomas Aquinas (a) strongly opposed the "double truth" theory, (b) distinguished but did not oppose faith and reason, which he said could never contradict each other, (c) synthesized Augustine and Aristotle wherever he could, (d) preferred Aristotle wherever he thought Aristotle was right and compatible with Christianity, and (e) refuted Aristotle by reason wherever he thought he was wrong and where he contradicted Christianity. As Augustine had "baptized" Plato, Aquinas "baptized" Aristotle.

## Reason, Faith, and Love

Bonaventure insists that reason must serve faith and, above all, love. Love is his absolute. He often uses the language of love, of the heart, of affection and passionate emotion. He says that **the best way to know God is by the experience of sweetness** [love and joy]; **this is more perfect, excellent and delightful than through rational inquiry."** This is a typical difference (but not quite a logical *contradiction*) between Bonaventure's typically Franciscan emphasis on the heart and Aquinas' more typically Dominican emphasis on the intellect.

Bonaventure's evaluation of human reason is, like Augustine's, quite pessimistic. He argues that our reason has been so darkened and weakened by the Fall into sin that it is bound to fall into error without correction by faith in divine revelation. This is why Aristotle, brilliant as he was, denied creation, providence, and immortality. Bonaventure compared pagan philosophers to ostriches, whose wings cannot fly into the heavens but whose legs can run very fast on the earth.

For Bonaventure man's mind is offered no less than four steps on its ladder of perfection that are higher than Aristotelian science: Platonic philosophical wisdom, Augustinian faith, the supernatural gifts of the Holy Spirit, and finally the "light of glory" in Heaven.

## Metaphysics

(1) *(Nature and Supernature)* Like Augustine, Bonaventure tends to minimize the role and power of creatures in order to maximize that of the Creator. Aquinas has the opposite tendency: to exalt the Creator precisely by exalting His creation, since "grace perfects nature rather than diminishing it." This difference is one of emphasis, not doctrine; tactics, not strategy; means, not ends. Both believe, love, and glorify the same Creator, but tend to have opposite emphases concerning creatures. Both believe that creatures are in

themselves good (since God made them) *and* that to us they are often temptations (since we tend to idolize them); but the two philosophers emphasize the two different halves of that common theological belief, and this produces some real philosophical disagreements.

Thus in his metaphysics Bonaventure "demotes" the role of secondary (created) causes by claiming that they do not really produce effects on their own without divine help. Effects emerge from the "seminal reasons" God put into the universe at creation, and are only catalyzed into existence, so to speak, by natural circumstances. Bonaventure is almost, but not quite, an "occasionalist." "Occasionalism" is the term given to the idea of Malebranche (ch. 59) in the seventeenth century that reduces all causality among creatures to "occasions" for divine activity; thus it is really only God that causes everything that happens. This was also the teaching of the Ash'arites among Muslim philosophers in the ninth century, and became Muslim orthodoxy among both Sunnis and Shi'ites. Its corollary was a radical demotion of the power of human reason and science.

This tendency appears also very clearly in Bonaventure's Augustinian epistemology of "divine illumination" (see ch. 36), which tends to a skepticism of merely human knowledge, and also in his ethics of the impotence of merely human virtue: without supernatural help, man cannot be even naturally good. Aquinas would not deny this in practice but would defend the natural order more in principle.


(2) *("Vertibility")* Another example of this tendency to demote the natural order is Bonaventure's teaching that the world is so radically contingent on God's will that it has no tendency to continue and would disappear into nothingness if God did not supernaturally preserve it continually. For everything tends to revert to that out of which it was made, and the universe was made "ex nihilo," out of nothing. He called this tendency of every creature to sink into nothingness its "vertibility."

Aquinas, though he believed in divine providence and preservation, did not believe in "vertibility" but believed that human souls, angels, and the universe, once they were created, by nature continued forever unless supernaturally annihilated by God.


(3) *(The Eternity of the World)* Aristotle claimed to prove that the universe was eternal, not created. Bonaventure countered with the following argument: (a) Each year, day, or second adds one unit of time to the past. (b) If the world had no beginning in time, an infinite amount of years, days, or seconds must have passed already. (c) But it is impossible to add to what is infinite. (d) Therefore, since it *is* possible to add to time, time is not infinite, i.e., the world is not eternal but has a temporal beginning.

(Aquinas thought that both this argument against the eternity of the world and Aristotle's argument for it were was rationally inconclusive, and held that only faith, not reason alone, could resolve this issue either way.)


(4) *(Exemplarism)* Here is an idea present in most medieval philosophers (e.g., Aquinas) but emphasized especially by Bonaventure: that all things are *signs* of God.

To see this point, remember that words and the concepts they express are not things but signs; they point beyond themselves to something else, to real things. (The later technical term among philosophers for this feature of words is "intentionality": signs "intend" or refer to things.) There are three possible views about the relation between words and things:

(a) Common sense says that *things* (like rocks or lions) *are not signs,* but that *words* (like "rocks" or "lions") *are.*

(b) The medieval Christian worldview says that *things are also signs*, since God created them according to His wisdom, i.e., the divine Ideas, which are one in His Logos or (mental) Word. They are different ways the infinite perfection of God can be imitated by finite creatures. Everything in the world symbolizes something in God. E.g., rocks point to God in their solidity and reliability; lions in their royalty, roses in their beauty. The medievals often said that God wrote two books: scripture and nature. Seeing nature as a set of symbols requires not cleverness or calculation but an imaginative and intuitive art of sign "reading," like reading a symbolic poem: an art that was easy before the Fall into sin but now is like reading a book in a foreign language until God's revelation in scripture and in Christ illuminated His other revelation, in nature.

(c) The above philosophy expanded common sense. In contrast, the contemporary philosophy called Deconstructionism shrinks common sense: it *denies that even words are signs* that have a fixed and objective sign-ificance They are merely intellectual weapons of social power over other minds. (Cf. ch. 89.)

Bonaventure distinguished three degrees of likeness to God: mere shadows, vestiges, and images (which are human souls). The medievals loved distinctions and hierachies.

He sees traces of the Trinity everywhere: e.g., form, matter & substance; the three dimensions of space; and memory, understanding and will in the soul.

### Reason's Road to God

This explains why, like St. Francis, Bonaventure emphasizes not logical proofs of God's existence but the purified mind's intuitive "seeing" God's presence everywhere.

He maintained that all men have an innate idea of God as a perfect, eternal being; and that this idea or essence immediately implied His existence. His boldly simple summary of St. Anselm's "ontological argument" is: "If God is God, God exists." His point is not the irrefutability of the argument's formal logic but that our innate idea of God is God's own presence to our intellect. His answer to the common critique of Anselm's argument, that Anselm leaps from God's essence (or idea) to existence, is that there *is* no leap, no gap between the two at all in reality, so there should not be such a gap in our concept either.

His most famous and popular book is a short mystical classic, *Itinerarium Mentis in Deum* (*The Itinerary of the Mind's Journey to God*), in which he maps the highly symbolic metaphysics of the universe as a Jacob's ladder by which our mind can climb, in steps, to God. The journey's strategy is the Augustinian and Platonic one of "upward via inward," **or from the external [physical] to the internal [spiritual] and from the temporal to the eternal.**

## Epistemology

(1) Bonaventure combines Augustinian "divine illumination" with Aristotelian "abstraction" by using abstraction to explain our knowledge of nature and illumination to explain our knowledge of our own souls and God (both of which he claims are known without the aid of the senses).

(2) He uses Augustine's notion of "the two faces of the soul": aided by the senses, the soul can turn downward and learn about the material world, as Aristotle explains; but it can also turn upward from the senses and the external world and know itself; and what it finds within is another world, of spirit, far greater than the universe. This is where we meet ourselves and God, and establish life's most important relationship.

(3) Bonaventure refutes skepticism and establishes certainty for human knowledge by establishing two criteria for certainty—infallibility in the knowing subject and immutability in the known object—and then arguing that only God has both of these attributes. He concludes that whenever we know the truth with certainty, our minds are in contact with God and His "illumination" from behind, so to speak, just as whenever we see light we are contacting the beams of the sun, even if we are not looking at the sun itself. So certainty is grounded not in our own reason's native powers but only in divine illumination.

## Ethics

A similar de-emphasis on the natural characterizes Bonaventure's ethics. He argues that without divine grace man cannot acquire even the natural cardinal virtues of wisdom, courage, temperance, and justice, much less the supernatural theological virtues of faith, hope, and charity. We need a moral illumination of the will to choose the good just as we need an intellectual illumination of the mind to know the truth.

In all these areas, Bonaventure emphasizes practice more than theory. He argues that even if by nature and in principle man is capable of certainty and virtue, as Aquinas argues he is, yet in his actual life the need for divine grace is far more obvious and important.

## Selected Bibliography

*The Philosophy of St. Bonaventure* by Etienne Gilson

# 43. Al-Kindi (c. 801–873)

Al-Kindi was the earliest Muslim philosopher the West knew, and the first to popularize Greek philosophy in the Muslim world. He was not a terribly original philosopher, but he had an encyclopedic mind, which covered the whole field of Greek learning: philosophy, chemistry, logic, medicine, astronomy, arithmetic, geometry, and music. Once, he cured his neighbor's son's illness with music.

He lived in Baghdad during the time of the flourishing of Muslim culture during the "Dark Ages" in Europe. This culture included Greek philosophy through a circuitous route. When the Emperor Justinian, in 529, closed all the pagan schools in Greece in a fit of fundamentalism, the philosophers took their books and settled in Edessa, in Mesopotamia. When this school was also closed, they went to Persia and founded schools there. In Syria, scholars translated the basic works of Greek science and philosophy into Syriac. When Islam conquered the Near East, beginning in 622 (the "hegira," Muhammad's flight to Mecca), and Islam replaced Christianity in the region, the caliphs (successors to the Prophet Muhammad) brought these Syrian scholars to Baghdad and had the Syriac translations translated into Arabic. The most influential of these works were Neoplatonic syntheses of Plato and Aristotle. That is why Muslim philosophers never thought they had to choose between Plato and Aristotle.

However, they had to choose between philosophy and Islam, largely because of the work of the next major Muslim philosopher, Al Ash'ari, as we shall see in the next chapter.

Al-Kindi, however, taught that although the Qur'an, as divine revelation, was infinitely superior to all human speculation, and although a purely rational, speculative theology was to be distrusted, yet Greek learning was compatible with the Qur'an.

The main idea Al-Kindi transmitted to subsequent Muslim philosophers was a peculiar reinterpretation of what Aristotle called the "agent intellect." For Aristotle this was simply the intellectual power of each individual soul to actively abstract universal forms from individual material substances. But for Al-Kindi it was a single spiritual substance, an Intelligence, like an angel, distinct from the soul and acting on it from above. Thus, man's mind is reduced to passivity. All universal concepts flow into our mind from a single angelic Mind. This idea was believed by nearly all Muslim philosophers to be Aristotle's teaching, and would cause much theological discombobulation and controversy among Muslim, and later Christian, theologians.

# 44. Al-Ash'ari (d. 936)

Al-Ash'ari is the first influential Muslim philosopher and, in at least one crucial way, the definitive one, for the mainline school of Muslim philosophy, the "Ash'arite," is named after him.

In the ninth century the "mutazilite" school, following Al-Kindi, emphasized the need to resort to reason to understand and properly interpret the divine revelation of the Qur'an. They also taught that there was an objective good and evil that reason could discover, and that God's will was always rational and just. They took Socrates' side in the dispute with Euthyphro, denying that an act was good only because God willed it. They denied that "might makes right" even for God, as was taught by another school of thought, the "mutakalimoun," which arose in reaction against the "mutazilites."

Al-Ash'ari taught for years as a mutazilite, then publicly renounced it and converted to the side of the mutakalimoun, insisting on the total freedom of God to will *anything*. His theological school, the Ash'arites, became mainline orthodoxy in Islam. From this time on there has always been a troubled relationship between Islam and Greek philosophy, with most Muslims repudiating Greek philosophy for the sake of religious orthodoxy and others, like Averroes, reinterpreting the Qur'an in light of Aristotle and treating Islam as inferior to Greek philosophy. But there was no Muslim Aquinas taking a third position and reinterpreting Greek philosophy in light of the Qur'an rather than vice versa, as Aquinas and Augustine reinterpreted Greek philosophy in light of the Bible.

The main doctrines of Al-Ash'ari and the Ash'arites are:

(1) That God's will is so free that it is not subject to reason.

(2) That an act is good only because God wills it, not because of its own nature. With God, "might makes right."

(3) That events in time are all caused directly by God, not by each other ("Occasionalism").

(4) That faith totally trumps reason, and that there should be no attempt at any synthesis between the Qur'an and philosophy.

# 45. Al-Farabi (c. 870–950)

Al-Farabi was a Persian Sufi mystic, born in Turkistan. His teacher was a Christian Aristotelian from Syria. But he was also a logician, and considered Aristotle the greatest mind in history. In fact he was nicknamed "the second master," after Aristotle. He wrote a creative commentary on Aristotle, synthesizing or reconciling him with Plato (really Plotinus), *The Harmonization of the Two Sages, the Divine Plato and Aristotle*. Medieval writers attributed over 100 books to him.

He interpreted the Qur'an as a book of culturally relative symbols, which was the highest form of thought non-philosophers could attain, but thought of philosophy as superior. He identified Allah with Plotinus's "The One," said that the Qur'an's "Paradise" is only symbolic, questioned individual immortality, and said the world is eternal, as Aristotle taught, even though Allah created it.

He is known mainly as being the first person ever to formulate the distinction which for Thomas Aquinas and others is perhaps the single most important distinction in philosophy, or at least in metaphysics: the distinction between essence and existence.

It was a philosophical way of stating the contingency of all creatures; that nothing except God has to be, or exists necessarily, or exists by its own nature (essence). They exist only by being caused to exist, by receiving existence from the Creator, i.e., the giver-of-existence. This Creator, on the other hand, exists necessarily, by His own essence, and needs no external cause. This is why He has no beginning. He also has no ending: He cannot lose His existence, as contingent creatures can.

To make this point, Al-Farabi commented on a remark of Aristotle's. Aristotle did not see the implications of this logical distinction for metaphysics: that the idea of *what a thing is* does not include *that it is*. The first is expressed in a concept, the second in a judgment. Al-Farabi carried this distinction from logic into metaphysics.

He did this by classifying existence as an "accident." (In Aristotelian language, everything must be either a substance or an accident.)

Aquinas later would deny both that existence is included in essence (for anything except God) *and* that it was an accident. He would say that unlimited existence is the supreme perfection and actuality, and is the essence of God, while finite essences are really metaphysically negative; they limit existence, rather as a wire limits electrical power or riverbanks limit a river.

Why did Al-Farabi and other Muslim and Christian philosophers extend Aristotle's logical distinction between concepts and judgments to the metaphysical distinction between essence and existence? Evidently, it came from their prior belief in God's creation of the universe out of nothing, a notion that originated only in Judaism and was unknown and unthinkable to the Greeks. Thus, ironically, the answer came before the question: the insight into the metaphysical contingency of the world—expressed by the profoundly new metaphysical question "Why does anything at all exist, rather than nothing?"—was elicited only by a prior belief in the answer ("It was created").

# 46. Avicenna (Ibn Sina) (980–1037)

## Life

The most important and influential of all Muslim philosophers, especially to medieval Christians, Avicenna used but surpassed the work of his two predecessors Al-Kindi and Al Farabi. He wrote one of his books at a rate of 50 pages a day while in hiding from an assassin. He wrote 450 books, said before he died, **I prefer a short life with width to a narrow one with length,** and died of too vigorous sex and too much opium.

## Faith and Reason

Like most Muslim philosophers and unlike most other Muslims, Avicenna reinterpreted Muhammad through Aristotle rather than vice versa. He affirmed that the Qur'an was infallible divine revelation but interpreted it symbolically rather than literally where it clashed with Aristotle. He maintained that rational philosophy and religious faith in the Qur'an do not contradict each other; in fact, they teach the same truth. But philosophy teaches it literally and the Qur'an only symbolically (though infallibly); in this way reason is superior to faith, Aristotle is superior to the Qur'an, and philosophers are superior to ordinary believers who depend on their imagination rather than their reason.

This pattern is a common one: religious rationalists (1) separate rather than marrying faith and reason, as Augustine and Aquinas did; and, to that end, they (2) distinguish two not only different but opposite interpretations of their religious data: the esoteric vs. the exoteric, that of their own scholarly minds vs. that of ordinary believers' lower and more imagination-dependent minds. This pattern is found in almost all religions and cultures. It is congenial to mystical religions like Hinduism and Buddhism, where it is mainline thinking; but it was resisted by traditional Jewish and Christian philosophers like Aquinas. (See ch. 50.) Because of the triumph of Al Ash'ari and the Ash'arites, it was not resisted in Islamic philosophy, though some (especially Averroes, ch. 48) carried it significantly farther than others.

For instance, Averroes taught that philosophy shows that the resurrection of the body, announced by Muhammad, cannot be rationally proved. Philosophy also disproves the material pleasures promised to the good and material pains promised to the evil after death. What awaits philosophers after death is the higher happiness of the union of their personal "potential (or passive) intellects" with the supreme truth in the single Agent Intellect.

Here is a list of religious heresies (ideas that contradict the data of the scriptures) in the teaching of Avicenna:

(1) The God of the Qur'an (Allah) is interpreted as The One of Plotinus. Though He is transcendent, since He alone is necessary and eternal, everything about Him is necessary, including His creating contingent beings. Creation is not His free choice.

(2) Where there is no free choice in God, there is none in man either. The logical consequence is that individual moral responsibility has to take second place to a kind of fatalism.

(3) God is so totally One that He cannot create the many. He can only create one being, which is a single spirit, angel, or Intellect. This being, in turn, creates a third spirit, etc. Nine spirits are thus "created" (really, emanated, as in Plotinus (ch. 33)), and these nine spirits move the nine celestial spheres defined in Aristotelian astronomy. (These were thought to contain the sun, moon, stars, and planets and to revolve around the earth.) The lowest is the spirit that moves the moon.

This cosmology was the "up-to-date" science of the time. It was a mixture of Aristotle and Neoplatonism. There is an obvious historical lesson here about the way to connect faith and science, at least for all those who believe their religion contains a revelation from an eternal God: when we think to stand on the fixed land of current science in order to map the moving waters of the sea of religious revelation, we make the double mistake of absolutizing the relative and relativizing the absolute. If, on the other hand, religion, which is about eternal things, is less time-bound than science, which is about temporal things, then the opposite is true.

(4) In the sublunary ("under the moon") world, the tenth spirit or Intelligence is the single Agent Intellect for all men.

(5) This Intellect, rather than God, also creates the four material elements and also individual human souls.

(6) All this happens of eternal necessity, not by the will and knowledge of God.

(7) Since the universe is necessary, it is eternal, as Aristotle taught. It always was.

(8) Also, since it is necessary, it is as good as it can possibly be. It is (as Leibnitz would later argue) "the best of all possible worlds."

(9) As Aristotle taught, God's providence does not extend to the inferior sublunary creation. To avoid the "blob God" of pantheism Avicenna posits the "snob God" of deism.

Most non-philosophical Muslim thinkers, of course, resisted these heresies, as did Christian thinkers who discovered them three centuries later in the rediscovered writings of Aristotle and his Muslim Neoplatonic interpreters. But Muslim thinkers resisted the very enterprise of rational philosophy that was the source of these heresies, while most Christian thinkers (especially Aquinas) used rational philosophy, under the light of their religious faith, to correct its own errors rationally.

## Metaphysics

Avicenna has a more complete philosophical system than any other Muslim philosopher. He wrote detailed and brilliant treatises on Aristotelian physics, astronomy, anthropology, logic, linguistics, cosmology, epistemology, and metaphysics. But the single most important influence of Avicenna on Aquinas and other Christian "Scholastic" philosophers was the distinction between essence and existence that he inherited from Al Farabi.

# 47. Al-Ghazali (1058–1111)

Al-Ghazali is probably the most readable of all Muslim philosophers, because he was not only a philosopher but also a mystic; because he wanted to be a saint more than he wanted to be a philosopher; and because he wrote a dramatic and personal intellectual autobiography, *The Deliverance from Error*, as well as a polemical book *The Incoherence of the Philosophers*, which was his refutation of the heretical teachings of Avicenna. *The Incoherence of the Philosophers* would elicit a reply from Averroes entitled *The Incoherence of Incoherence*.

Excerpts from his spiritual autobiography show striking similarities to Augustine and Descartes:

**Inherited beliefs lost their hold on me when I was still quite young. . . . For I saw that the children of Christians always grew up embracing Christianity, and the children of Jews always grew up adhering to Judaism, and the children of Muslims always grew up following the religion of Islam . . .**

**I would dive daringly into the depths of this profound sea . . . pounce upon every problem, and dash into every mazy difficulty . . . with the aim of discriminating between truth and error, and between the faithful follower of tradition and the heterodox innovator . . .**

**I then scrutinized all my cognitions and found myself devoid of any knowledge that was secure except sense data and self-evident truths . . .**

**I began to reflect on my sense data to see if I could make myself doubt them. This protracted effort to induce doubt finally brought me to the point where my soul would not allow me to admit safety from error even in the case of my sense data. Rather it began to be open to doubt about them . . . sight looks at a star and sees it as something small . . . the sense judge makes its judgment but the reason judge refutes them . . .**

**Then I said . . . perhaps I can rely only on those rational . . . primary truths such as our asserting that ten is more than three, and one and the same thing cannot be simultaneously affirmed and denied. . . . Then sense data spoke up: What assurance have you that your reliance on rational data is not like your reliance on sense data?**

**. . . Don't you see that when you are asleep you believe certain things and imagine certain circumstances and believe they are fixed and lasting and entertain no doubts about that being their status? Then you wake up and know that all your imaginings and beliefs were groundless and insubstantial. So while everything you**

believe through sensation or intellection in your waking state may be true in relation to that state, what assurance have you that you may not suddenly experience a state which would have the same relation to your waking state as the latter has to your dreaming? . . .

This malady was mysterious and it lasted for nearly two months. During that time I was a skeptic in fact but not in utterance and doctrine. At length God Most High cured me of that sickness. My soul regained its health and equilibrium and once again I accepted the self-evident data of reason and relied on them with safety and certainty. But that was not achieved by constructing a proof or putting together an argument. On the contrary, it was the effect of a light which God Most High cast into my breast. And that light is the key to most knowledge. Therefore whoever thinks that the unveiling of truth depends on precisely formulated proofs has indeed straitened the broad mercy of God . . .

Philosophers . . . can be divided into three main divisions: Materialists, Naturalists, and Theists. The first category, the Materialists, were a group of the most ancient philosophers who denied the existence of the omniscient and omnipotent Creator-Ruler. They alleged that the world existed from eternity as it is, of itself and not by reason of a Maker. Animals have unceasingly come from seed, and seed from animals; thus it was, and thus it ever will be. These are the godless in the full sense of the term.

The second category, the Naturalists, were men who devoted much study to the world of nature. . . . In these they saw such marvels of God Most High's making and such wonders of His wisdom that they were compelled . . . to acknowledge the existence of a wise Creator cognizant of the aims and purposes of all things. Indeed, no one can study the science of anatomy and the marvelous uses of the organs without acquiring this compelling knowledge of the perfect governance of Him Who shaped the structure of animals, and especially that of man.

However, it appeared to these philosophers . . . that man's rational power was dependent on the mixture of his humors (chemicals) and that its corruption would follow upon the corruption of the mixture of his humors, and so that power would cease to exist . . . consequently they denied the afterlife . . .

The third category, the Theists, were the later philosophers such as Socrates, master of Plato, and Plato, master of Aristotle . . .

It is in the metaphysical sciences that most of the philosophers' errors are found . . . in three of which they must be taxed with unbelief. . . . It was to refute their doctrine . . . that we composed our book *The Incoherence.*

In the three questions first mentioned they were opposed to the belief of all Muslims, viz. in their affirming (1) that men's bodies will not be assembled on the Last day. . . , (2) their declaration "God Most High knows universals but not particulars". . . , (3) their maintaining the eternity of the world . . .

When I had finished with the science of philosophy—having mastered and understood it and pinpointed its errors—I knew that philosophy also was inadequate to satisfy my aim fully. I also realized that reason alone is incapable of fully grasping all problems or of getting to the heart of all difficulties. . . .

. . . the way of the Sufis . . . is to lop off all the obstacles present in the soul and to rid oneself of its reprehensible habits and vicious qualities in order to attain thereby a heart empty of all save God . . . it became clear to me that their most distinctive characteristic is something that can be attained not by study but rather by experience . . .

I also considered my activities—the best of them having been public and private instruction—and saw that in them I was applying myself to sciences unimportant and useless in this pilgrimage to the hereafter. Then I reflected on my intention in my public teaching, and I saw that it was not directed purely to God, but rather was instigated and motivated by the quest for fame. . . . I set about mending my ways . . .

I would put one foot forward and the other backward. In the morning I would have a sincere desire to seek the things of the afterlife, but by evening the hosts of passion would assail it and render it lukewarm. Mundane desires began tugging me with their chains to remain as I was, while the herald of faith was crying out: Away! Up and away! Only a little is left of your life, and a long journey lies before you! All the theory and practice in which you are involved is eye service and fakery! If you do not prepare now for the afterlife, when will you do so? . . .

I incessantly vacillated between the contending pull of worldly desires and the appeals of the afterlife for about six months. . . . God put a lock upon my tongue so that I was impeded from public teaching . . . my tongue would not utter a single word . . . I could neither swallow nor digest . . . the physicians lost hope of treating me . . .

Then, when I perceived my powerlessness . . . I had recourse to God Most High . . . and I was answered by Him Who "answers the needy man when he calls on Him," and He made it easy for my heart to turn away from fame and fortune . . .

I departed from Baghdad after I had distributed what wealth I had, laying by only the amount needed for my support and the sustenance of my children. . . . I entered Damascus and resided there for nearly two years. My only occupation was seclusion and solitude and spiritual exercise and combat . . .

I knew with certainty that the Sufis are those who uniquely follow the way to God Most High; their mode of life is best of all, their way the most direct of ways, and their ethic the purest. . . . Its purity—the first of its requirements—is the total purification of the heart from everything other than God Most High. Its key . . . is the utter absorption of the heart in the remembrance of God. Its end is being completely lost in God.

# 48. Averroes (1126–1198)

His real name was Ibn Rushd (which sounds like a student's excuse for not finishing an exam). He was a Spanish Arab born in Cordova. His (Aristotelianly-faithful) commentaries on Aristotle earned him the nickname "The Commentator" among medieval philosophers. He influenced Western Christian philosophers more than any other Muslim except Avicenna, and provoked them more, by his thoroughly Aristotelian reinterpretation of those Qur'anic (and Biblical) teachings about God and the soul that contradicted Aristotle. Averroes was labeled a heretic by the Islamic authorities and banished from his native Cordova, but was eventually welcomed back.

## Faith and Reason

Averroes' esoterism (look it up!) is based on his classification of three essentially diverse kinds of human minds.

First, there are "men of demonstration," i.e., philosophers, who can comprehend and demand logical proofs, which are necessary.

Second, there are theologians, who are "dialectical men" who are satisfied with rational arguments that are only probable or fitting to support their faith by reasoning. Reason is fully mature in the first class, and in a childlike condition in the second class.

But it is not even yet awake in the third class, which is the vast majority of men. These are "men of exhortation," who respond to rhetoric and oratory, which appeals not to reason but to the passions and the imagination. They are not called upon to understand their faith intellectually, but only to hear preachers' exhortations and to live virtuously.

The philosophers do not need faith and religion, since they are virtuous for purely rational motives. But since religion and philosophy work for the same end (virtue), they are allies in practice, even when they seem theoretically to contradict each other. The beliefs of the masses are simply philosophical truths adapted to inferior minds.

Averroes does not despise these inferior minds, for they can be practically wise and saintly, though they cannot be philosophically wise and rational. He criticizes the second class, the theologians, for mingling faith and reason. Averroes affirms that Moses, Jesus, and Muhammad were prophets sent by God to teach truth concretely, symbolically, and imaginatively to the masses who could not understand the higher truths of abstract, rational philosophy.

To resolve the disputes among the different schools of Muslim theology, Averroes wants each of these three kinds of minds to have access to different kinds of writings. The masses should not study philosophy; it would upset their faith. They should study only the Qur'an, which alone is addressed to all three kinds of minds. (This proves its miraculous character.) It has both exoteric (literal and imaginative) and esoteric (philosophical and logical) dimensions. Though there seem to be contradictions between its teachings and the teachings of philosophy (i.e., Aristotle, whom Averroes regarded as the absolute pinnacle of all possible human wisdom, **"the ultimate in human perfection"**), all disputes will cease if the three levels of interpretation are sharply distinguished. Philosophical minds alone understand absolute truth absolutely. Ordinary people should not be taught philosophy; it would upset their simple faith. Their religion is not literally true, but it is a social necessity to keep order and virtue among the masses. (It is a sort of Santa Claus story to make those who are intellectually childlike happy and good.)

The theoretical contradictions between philosophy (Aristotle) and religion (the Qur'an, interpreted literally) are essentially the same as those in Avicenna. The most important of them are:

(1) The universe as eternal and necessary, not created.

(2) God as necessary, not free.

(3) The denial of divine providence.

(4) The denial that individual men have their own agent intellects or even their own potential (passive, possible) intellects. (Avicenna had given man at least that.) Man is thus merely a superior animal, and totally mortal.

(5) Since individual human souls are mortal, there is no Last Judgment, Heaven, or Hell.

Having denied creation (point [1] above), Averroes also naturally denied the real distinction between essence and existence. The fact that Aristotle did not teach this metaphysical doctrine is enough to prove to Averroes that it has no place in philosophy.

"Latin Averroism" is the name historians give to the influence of Averroes' teachings on Christian philosophers in the West. This influence was stemmed above all by St. Thomas Aquinas. Renaissance painters often depict Averroes groveling under Aquinas's feet, similar to paintings and statues of Satan groveling under the feet of St. Michael the Archangel.

# 49. Moses Maimonides (1135–1204)

Moses ben Maimon was the greatest medieval Jewish philosopher and theologian. Born in Cordova, and taught Torah and Talmud by his father, his family was forced to leave Spain when he was thirteen, when the period of peaceful coexistence among Jews, Muslims, and Christians ended. His family settled in Cairo. He was a jeweler, a doctor, and the court physician to Saladin. He became the chief Rabbi of Egypt. He was educated by Muslim teachers, who taught the metaphysics, cosmology, and anthropology of Aristotle at a time when Aristotle was unknown in Christendom except for his logic. This was an Aristotle synthesized with elements in Neoplatonism as interpreted especially by Avicenna and Averroes.

Like Thomas Aquinas, Maimonides presented his opponents' objections very fairly and strongly—so much so that some rabbis worried that readers who read only the objections and then fell asleep would wake up as heretics.

## Faith and Reason

Jewish philosophers confronted the same issue as Muslim and Christian philosophers about the relation between faith and reason. The issue's name was Aristotle. The greatest mind in history seemed to contradict these three religions on a number of issues, most importantly (1) the creation of the world and time, (2) divine providence, and (3) individual immortality, all of which Aristotle denied were possible. For him (1) the world was eternal, (2) God would pollute His perfection if He cared for inferior creatures, and (3) souls, being only the forms of bodies, died with bodies.

Muslim philosophers all opted for either (a) a reinterpretation of these Qur'anic doctrines as non-literal and a distinction between exoteric religious truth (the Qur'an) and esoteric philosophical truth, which was higher, or (b) a fundamentalist reaction against this, and the insistence that God and His will simply transcended reason.

It was a dramatic moment in intellectual history: would the three Western religions be overwhelmed by Greek philosophy? Would they fear and reject it, or could they reinterpret and assimilate it? Maimonides, like Bonaventure, Aquinas, and Scotus after him, and unlike most Muslims, taught the third position: that reason and faith do not and cannot conflict, and that all apparent conflicts result from misunderstandings or misinterpretations of either philosophy or scripture (e.g., taking anthropomorphic figures of speech about God literally). And this did not involve weakening or "demythologizing" of the faith, or an esoteric-vs.-exoteric "double truth" theory. Maimonides is a firmly orthodox Jew and also an Aristotelian philosopher. He wrote his classic *Guide for the*

*Perplexed* precisely for those who were perplexed by the apparent conflicts between the two, to show that these conflicts were not necessary. To do this, philosophical arguments were necessary; reason could be defended, and reconciled with faith, only by reason.

All this, both the strategy and the tactics, is similar to the work of Aquinas, who was in fact strongly and positively influenced by "Rabbi Moses." Maimonides' writings, however, do not have the systematic order and logical rigor of Aquinas's.

## The Specific Issues

The most prominent issue was the biblical idea of creation vs. the Greek idea of the eternity of the world. Aristotle thought he had proved the necessity of the eternity of the world. Maimonides, like Aquinas after him, showed that he had not; that philosophy cannot resolve the issue, so that faith's answer, though it cannot be proved by reason alone, does not contradict reason. For Aristotle had assumed, in his argument, that God's power is limited.

On divine providence he shows that the Bible is actually more reasonable than Aristotle, since a God who knows only universals and not individuals (Aristotle's God) is intellectually inferior, not superior, to a God who knows both (the God of the Bible); and that a God who is only the final cause of the universe but not its efficient cause (Aristotle's God) is metaphysically inferior, not superior, to a God who is both (the God of the Bible). He also argues that Providence is evident in nature's details.

On immortality, Maimonides is halfway between Aristotle and Aquinas, with his notion that each of us acquires, by divine justice, a kind of mental capital, an investment, by his acts of virtue in this world, which increase his merit and his reward after death, namely the degree of the intellectual vision of God; so that it depends on each of us to save and eternalize as much of himself as possible by enriching his mind through studying and practicing true philosophy. (Perhaps this is closer to Spinoza than to Aristotle: cf. ch. 60.)

Maimonides also taught
(1) that Intelligences are wholly free from matter;
(2) that the soul is the form of the body;
(3) that we each have our individual passive intellect;
(4) but there is one agent intellect, which illuminates all minds;
(5) that reason can prove the existence of God as (a) Unmoved Mover, (b) Primary efficient cause, and (c) necessary being (the first three of Aquinas's famous "five ways" are strongly influenced by Maimonides);
(6) that we can know only what God is not, not what God is;
(7) that analogical knowledge of God is not positive knowledge at all;
(8) that the only name of God that is not relative to creatures is the self-revealed Tetragrammaton (sacred four-consonant word) "I AM," which means pure, absolute, necessary existence;

(9) that evil is explained by limitations inherent in finite creaturehood or by the rational creature's freely-chosen self-inflicted defects;

(10) that existence is distinct from essence;

(11) that it is an "accident" of essence, as Avicenna said; and

(12) that there are four hierarchical levels of human perfection: (a) material wealth, (b) bodily health, (c) moral virtue, and (d) the understanding of God. (Aquinas will agree with all but 4, 7, and 11.)

# 50. St. Thomas Aquinas (1225–1274)

"Thomists" are thinkers who consider themselves disciples of St. Thomas more than any other philosopher, i.e., they consider St. Thomas the wisest, most brilliant philosophical mind of all time. There have been more Thomists than Platonists, Aristotelians, Augustinians, Cartesians, Humeans, Kantians, Nietzscheans, Marxists, Heideggerians, or anything else in the history of philosophy. His philosophy has staying power. It is still a very live option 750 years later, and has shown itself capable of assimilating new philosophical developments like existentialism, phenomenology, and personalism as well as the discoveries of modern science.

Why?

### Reasons for Aquinas's Popularity

The first reason has to be telling the truth. That trumps all else.

The simple, direct, and common-sense nature of this first answer leads to a second: his thought is remarkably simple, direct, and, above all, commonsensical, even though it is expressed in abstract, technical, and difficult medieval-Aristotelian ("Scholastic") terminology. (That is the point of G. K. Chesterton's biography *St. Thomas Aquinas, the Dumb Ox,* which many Thomists regard as the greatest book ever written about St. Thomas.) Once you understand about a dozen Aristotelian terms, he is actually very easy to read.

Third, like Augustine he had a heart as well as a head. He was a saint and a practical man. Peasants, kings, and popes wrote to him for practical advice and always got it. (One example: his advice for dealing with depression: **a glass of wine, a hot bath, and a good night's sleep**.) Many of his theoretical points have practical life-changing applications.

Fourth, perhaps more than anyone else in history, he combined the two essential ideals of philosophical thought: exact logic and intuitive wisdom; clarity and profundity. He wrote clearly and simply about the most profound questions of God and man, life and death, good and evil, mind and will, soul and body, fate and freedom, virtue and vice, the natural and the supernatural. He always seems formidable on first reading and always becomes clearer and clearer on every subsequent rereading. He is a transparent window, with no emotional, ideological, or personal "baggage." Everything is "bottom line" and straight to the point. And nothing is asserted without definition, explanation, and proof.

Fifth, more completely than anyone else before or since, he synthesized or married faith and reason, Christianity and Greek philosophy, religion and science. (Philosophy is a "science" in the broad, pre-modern sense.) He had an inclusive rather than an exclusive mind. Within philosophy itself he synthesized insights from nearly every major philosopher before him.

Sixth, he was not only inclusive and synthetic but also very analytical. He combined careful, elaborate detail with "the big picture," cosmic sweep, or metaphysical "worldview."

Seventh, he was judicious and moderate, careful and patient to avoid opposite extremes and oversimplifications.

His philosophy reminds me of a Gothic cathedral, built up over centuries into a rich and complex variety in unity—like the universe itself. Edwin Panofsky, in his little classic *Gothic Architecture and Scholasticism,* showed this structural parallel in detail.

Many contemporary philosophies, by comparison, remind me of either dull apartment buildings or amusement parks.

## Aquinas's Life

Nietzsche claimed that every philosophical system is merely personal confession. At the opposite extreme, scholars often treat philosophies as if they were books that fell from the sky rather than from human beings who came from the earth. To navigate between these two extremes, I will tell some telling stories about Aquinas's life that reveal his personality.

Born the son of a rich and influential Italian count, he was a child prodigy, both in intelligence and sanctity. At age five he asked his teacher the stunningly simple question, **"What is God?"** and, not satisfied with his answer, decided to become a theologian to find out.

He once endured surgery without a tear (or an anesthetic). He feared only one thing: thunder. He had seen his sister killed by a lightning storm when he was very young.

His parents groomed him to become an Abbot in Christendom's most prestigious religious order (the Benedictines), eventually the abbot of their most famous monastery (Monte Cassino), and eventually perhaps the next Pope. But Aquinas, like a hippie teenager, ran away to join the new and not-yet-respectable teaching order of wandering, begging friars, the Dominicans (a sort of intellectual version of the Franciscans). To stop him, his brothers kidnapped him, locked him in a castle room, and sent in a prostitute to tempt him. He immediately seized a log from the fireplace, with which he quickly persuaded her to exit, and burned a cross on the door. Eventually, his family gave up. He had won the duel of wills.

He was very large. He walked thousands of miles across Europe rather than ride donkeys (which were too small for him) or horses (which were too rich for him).

He studied under St. Albert the Great, the most famous teacher in Christendom, an Aristotelian who focused on scientific questions. He was so shy, silent, and placid that his fellow students called him "the dumb ox." Albert, hearing this, said, prophetically, "You may call him a dumb ox, but I say his bellowing will be heard around the world."

As a theology professor at the University of Paris he loved the public debates (called "disputed questions") in which professors had to field unpredictable questions and objections from students and faculty, and do so in clear logical form. The format of the *Summa Theologiae* is not artificial but a natural summary of these debates.

He was very absent-minded. Once, required to be present at a banquet honoring the King of France (the wise and saintly Louis), ignoring the prestigious guests' conversation, he suddenly thought of an argument and smashed his fist on the table with glee, muttering, **"That will settle the Manichees!"** The wise king, instead of being insulted, called for his secretary to bring pen and paper to record it before it was forgotten.

Once, traveling over a mountain range, when the sun emerged to illumine a whole kingdom below, his traveling companion said, "Wouldn't it be grand to own all that you can see?" Aquinas replied, **"I'd rather own the missing page of that Aristotle manuscript."** In his scale of values, one page of truth trumped a kingdom.

Since he thought and spoke four times as fast as anyone could write, he wrote his two massive *Summas* by dictating to four secretaries at once, one sentence after another, with no revisions or second drafts. His own handwriting is hurried, scribbled, and hardly legible.

A few months before his death he refused to finish the *Summa Theologiae*, or to write any more at all, calling everything he had ever written "**straw**" compared with what he had seen, in mystical experience. Straw was used in the Middle Ages to cover animal dung. St. Paul used the same image in Philippians 3:8.

Shortly before his death he made a general confession of all the sins of his life. His confessor emerged from the confessional weeping, "The sins of a child of five!"

Here is the most revealing story of all. His fellow monks once found him prone on the floor of the chapel in the middle of the night in audible conversation with Christ on the crucifix, who said to him, "You have written well of me, Thomas; what will you have as your reward?" He answered simply, **"Only Yourself, Lord."** He would have said that those were the three most eloquent words of his life. The rest were "straw."

### Aquinas Compared with Augustine

As the essential comparison in ancient philosophy is between Plato and Aristotle, the essential comparison in medieval philosophy is between Augustine and Aquinas.

It is not so much a contrast doctrinally between a Christian Platonism and a Christian Aristotelianism as a contrast personally between two different sets of remarkable talents and temperaments. Augustine speaks from the depths, Aquinas from the heights. Augustine's insight is into man existential, Aquinas's is into man essential. Augustine is the master of metaphor, Aquinas of concepts. Augustine's head and heart are in a rich, stormy marriage; Aquinas's heart and head are in perfect, quiet unity.

Augustine has less practical confidence in human reason than Aquinas does because he knew from experience how wounded and self-deceptive it could be, while Aquinas was born, lived, and died in the light. This gives Augustine a richness and a passion but also a one-sidedness and a straining that contrasts with Aquinas's ease and balance. It is the playboy who wanted to do without God and grace, and who experienced the weakness of nature and natural reason, who shows us our own deepest needs, sufferings, and failures. It is the perfected saint who shows us the essential nature of God, ourselves, and our philosophical cosmos as clearly as anyone ever has.

Yet their teaching is essentially the same both in principle and in practice. The common principle is that grace and faith must precede and perfect nature and reason, but when it does, nature and reason are indeed perfected, not diminished. The common practice is that both enable our thought to be one with our prayer.

### Aquinas's Writings and How to Read Them

In his short, 25-year career he wrote tens of thousands of pages (over 8 million words, including 2 million commenting on the Bible and 1 million on Aristotle), in addition to his unfinished masterpiece, the *Summa Theologiae* ("summary of theology"). The *Summa* is not a closed system but an ordered summary, a mirror of reality, beginning in God, proceeding to creation, centering on man, and culminating in man's search for happiness and return to God, who is the Alpha and the Omega. Reality is seen as a kind of cosmic circulatory system, with the heart of God pumping the blood of being through the arteries of creation into the universe, which wears a human face, and receiving the cosmos back through the veins of man's free choices of moral virtue, faith, hope, and love.

Even if you are not a theologian, a Catholic, a Christian, or a theist, your mind will be powerfully exercised and improved by reading Aquinas. Read him slowly; it is more like reading Euclid than reading Dickens. It is like eating spinach: it may taste strange at first, but it makes you strong. His habits of clarity, order, and logic rub off, even when you disagree with him. He is always scrupulously fair. Though his style is utterly prosaic compared to Augustine's, his "fanatical" honesty and passion for truth is similar. A CIA agent recruiting for spies among philosophers would find no two more hopelessly inept liars than these two.

The basic unit of the *Summa* is the "article," which is a summary of a debate. It is typically one to three pages long, and contains five parts, all of which are necessary for a complete logical treatment:

(1) The question is formulated in a Yes or No (pro/con) format. (**"Whether . . ."**)

(2) All the major objections to Aquinas's answer are stated as clearly and strongly and fairly as possible. (**"It seems that . . ."**)

(3) An argument from a past authority for Aquinas's answer is given (**"On the contrary . . ."**)

(4) The main body of the article then defines terms, explains presuppositions, and proves its conclusion with syllogisms. ("**I answer that . . .**")

(5) Each objection is answered, usually by distinguishing two meanings of ambiguous terms, thus perceiving half-truths in each objection. ("**I respond . . .**")

Like the Socratic dialog, it is an eminently imitable format.*

## Faith and Reason

Aquinas was primarily a theologian. Philosophy, for him, as for most of the medievals, was an indispensable aid to theology, as mathematics is an indispensable aid to physics. "***Philosophia ancilla theologiae***"—philosophy the serving-maid to theology—was a common medieval slogan or formula.

Theology is a "science" in the older, broader sense: a rationally organized body of knowledge by causes. Theology was the science (*logos*) of God (*theos*), and two kinds of it were distinguished. "Natural theology" was based on what could be discovered, understood, and demonstrated (the three "acts of the mind") by human reason alone. That division of Aristotle's metaphysics in which he speculated about God is an example of "natural theology." "Revealed theology" was based on divine revelation, i.e., on the faith ( belief) that God had spoken in Christ, in Christ's Church, and in the Church's Scripture, and revealed to man things man could never have discovered, understood, or proved by his own unaided human reason—e.g., that He is a Trinity, and that His love for man was so great that it moved him to sacrifice His Son for man's salvation.

"Faith" thus meant two things for Aquinas. It could mean (1) the human act of belief in this divine revelation.**Or it could mean (2) its objects, i.e., all the truths revealed by God to man and known to man by faith in sense (1). When Aquinas compares faith and reason, he compares not two psychological acts (1) but two bodies of truths (2). Faith is a kind of knowledge, not a kind of feeling. It is like Baby believing Mommy when Mommy says it's dangerous to play with fire. (Only someone without reason or without humility would find this comparison insulting. For if God exists at all, it is certainly reasonable to think He is at least as superior to us as Mommy is to Baby.)

Aquinas distinguishes three kinds of truths: (1) those knowable only by faith (e.g., the Trinity), (2) those knowable only by reason, since God did not reveal them (e.g., 2+2=4, owls hoot, and the universe is 14 billion years old), and (3) truths that are knowable by unaided reason but which God also revealed to us because of the weakness

---

* Cf. *Summa Philosophica* by Peter Kreeft.
** N.B. Faith is correlative to divine revelation as sight is correlative to color or desire to desirability; it is relative to its object. It is not simply a psychological attitude, as it often is taken to be in modern thought. Similarly, the modern concept of "consciousness" as a mental world in itself simply does not exist in medieval thought. Instead, there is "knowledge," which is essentially "intentional," i.e., it always intends some object, real or imaginary

of our minds (e.g., that He exists, is one, is good, and that happiness requires moral virtue). Think of two interlocking circles; label one "faith" and one "reason."

Aquinas then argues that **although the truth of the Christian faith . . . surpasses the capacity of the reason, nevertheless that truth which the human reason is naturally endowed to know cannot be opposed to the truth of the Christian faith . . . for only the false is opposed to the true . . . therefore it is impossible that the truth of faith should be opposed to those true principles that human reason naturally knows. Furthermore, that which is introduced into the soul of the student by the teacher is contained in the knowledge of the teacher. . . . Now the knowledge of rational principles that are naturally known to us has been implanted in us by God, for God is the author of our nature. These principles, therefore, are also contained by the divine Wisdom. Hence, whatever contradicts them contradicts the divine Wisdom and therefore cannot come from Gd. Therefore that which we know by faith to be divinely revealed cannot be contrary to our natural knowledge.**

In other words, in the words of Arthur Holmes, "all truth is God's truth."

Aquinas richly joins philosophy and theology and, within theology, faith and reason, but without confusing the two, as a marriage joins a man and a woman. In the *Summa Theologiae* every argument tells you what its premises are, and the very structure of each "article" distinguishes premises based on faith and authority (the "On the contrary" section) and premises based on reason (the "I answer that" section). In the *Summa Contra Gentiles,* the first three books concern truths that can be attained by reason alone while the fourth book concerns truths like the Trinity, the Incarnation, and the Sacraments, that are known by faith alone.

## The Existence of God

The most famous of all arguments for the existence of God are Aquinas's "five ways" in the *Summa Theologiae* (I,2,3). They are abbreviated summaries of longer, more complex arguments—e.g., the first "way" takes only one paragraph in the *Summa Theologiae* but 21 paragraphs in the *Summa Contra Gentiles*.

Their common strategy is to begin with an empirical observation of some feature of the world: ("motion," i.e., change; coming-into-being, contingency [ability to go out of existence], degrees of perfection, and order), then use the principle of causality* to prove that these empirical phenomena are not explainable unless there is a First,

---

* This principle is almost the very definition of reason and order, for it is the commonest of all ways to explain things everywhere: in science, in philosophy, and in common sense. Aquinas regarded this principle as metaphysical, not just psychological or epistemological, i.e., as not just a mental concept that we impose on things to explain them but as objectively and universally true and knowable. Nothing "just happens," nothing can begin to exist without a sufficient cause of its existence.

Un-caused Cause—which is one of the unique properties of God. The five proofs correspond to five kinds of causality: cause of motion (change), cause of existence, cause of necessity, cause of degrees of perfection or goodness, and cause of order (teleological order to an end).)

In each case the essential argument is that if there is no First (un-caused) Cause, there could be no second (caused) causes, no matter how many these may be; but there are second causes; therefore there must be a First Cause. Thus we conclude to a being with five divine attributes: (1) unmoved mover, (2) uncaused cause of existence, (3) necessarily and eternally existent, (4) absolutely perfect standard of perfection, and (5) intelligent cause of order to an end.

The arguments are so famous that the article deserves to be quoted verbatim:

**S.T. I, 2, 3: Whether God exists?**

**Objection 1: It seems that God does not exist, because if one of two contraries be infinite, the other would be altogether destroyed; but the word "God" means that He is infinite goodness; if, therefore, God existed, there would be no evil discoverable. But there is evil in the world. Therefore God does not exist.**

**Objection 2: Further, it is superfluous to suppose that what can be accounted for by a few principles has been produced by many. But it seems that everything we see in the world can be accounted for by other principles, supposing God did not exist. For all natural things can be reduced to one principle, which is nature; and all voluntary things can be reduced to one principle, which is human reason or will. Therefore there is no need to suppose God's existence.**

**On the contrary, it is said in the person of God: "I am Who am." (Ex. 3:14.)**

**I answer that the existence of God can be proved in five ways.**

**The first and more manifest way is the argument from motion. It is certain and evident to our senses that in the world some things are in motion. Now whatever is in motion is put in motion by another, for nothing can be in motion except it is in potentiality to that towards which it is in motion, whereas a thing moves inasmuch as it is in act (actuality). Thus that which is actually hot, such as fire, makes wood, which is potentially hot, to be actually hot, and thereby moves and changes it. Now it is not possible that the same thing should be at once in actuality and potentiality in the same respect, but only in different respects. For what is actually hot cannot simultaneously be potentially hot, but it is potentially cold. It is therefore impossible that in the same respect and in the same way a thing should be both mover and**

moved, i.e., that it should move itself. Therefore whatever is in motion must be put in motion by another.

If that by which it is put in motion be itself put in motion, then this also must needs be put in motion by another, and that by another again. But this cannot go on (i.e., regress) to infinity, because then there would be no first mover and, consequently, no other mover, seeing that subsequent movers move only inasmuch as they are put in motion by the first mover, as the staff moves only because it is put in motion by the hand. Therefore it is necessary to arrive at a first mover, put in motion by no other; and this everyone understands to be God.

The second way is from the nature of the efficient cause. In the world of sense we find there is an order of efficient causes. There is no case now (neither is it, indeed, possible) in which a thing is found to be the efficient cause of itself; for so it would be prior to itself, which is impossible. Now in efficient causes it is not possible to go on to infinity, because in all efficient causes following in order, the first is the cause of the intermediate cause, and the intermediate is the cause of the ultimate cause, whether the intermediate cause be several or one only. Now to take away the cause is to take away the effect. Therefore, if there be no first cause among efficient causes, there will be no ultimate, nor any intermediate, cause. But if in efficient causes it is possible to go on to infinity, there will be no first efficient cause; neither will there be an ultimate effect, nor any intermediate efficient causes—all of which is plainly false. Therefore it is necessary to admit a first efficient cause, to which everyone gives the name of God.

The third way is taken from possibility and necessity, and runs thus. We find in nature things that are possible to be and [or] not to be, since they are found to be generated and to corrupt, and consequently they are possible both to be and not to be. But it is impossible for these always to exist, for that which is possible not to be, at some time is not. Therefore, if everything is possible not to be, then at one time there could have been nothing in existence. Now if this were true, even now there would be nothing in existence, because that which does not exist only begins to exist by [being caused by] something already existing. Therefore, if at one time nothing was in existence, it would have been impossible for anything to have begun to exist; and thus even now nothing would be in existence—which is absurd. Therefore, not all beings are merely possible, but there must exist something the existence of which is necessary . . .

But every necessary thing either has its necessity caused by another, or not. Now it is impossible to go on to infinity in necessary things which have their necessity caused by another, as has been already proved in regard to efficient causes. Therefore we cannot but postulate the existence of some being which has of itself its own necessity, and does not receive it from another, but rather causes in others their necessity. This all men speak of as God.

**The fourth way is taken from the gradation to be found in things. Among beings there are some more and some less good, true, noble, and the like. But "more" and "less" are predicated of different things according as they resemble in their different ways something which is the maximum, as a thing is said to be hotter according as it more nearly resembles that which is hottest. So there is something which is truest, something best, something noblest, and consequently something which is uttermost being. For those things that are greatest in truth are greatest in being, as it is written in *Metaphysics* II** (Aristotle). **Now the maximum in any genus is the cause of all in that genus, as fire, which is the maximum of heat, is the cause of all hot things. Therefore there must also be something which is to all beings the cause of their being, goodness, and every other perfection; and this we call God.**

**The fifth way is taken from the governance of the world. We see that things which lack intelligence, such as natural bodies, act for an end, and this is evident from their acting always, or nearly always, in the same way, so as to obtain the best result. Hence it is plain that not fortuitously but designedly do they achieve their end. Now whatever lacks intelligence cannot move towards an end unless it be directed by some being with knowledge and intelligence, as the arrow is shot to its mark by the archer. Therefore some intelligent being exists by whom all natural things are directed to their end; and this being we call God.**

**Reply to Objection 1: As Augustine says** (Enchiridion 11), **"Since God is the highest good, He would not allow any evil to exist in His works unless His omnipotence and goodness were such as to bring good even out of evil." This is part of the infinite goodness of God, that He should allow evil to exist and out of it produce good.**

**Reply to Objection 2: Since nature works for a determinate end under the direction of a higher agent, whatever is done by nature must be traced back to God, as to its first cause. So also whatever is done voluntarily must also be traced back to some higher cause other than human reason and will, since these can change and fail. For all things that are changeable and capable of defect must be traced back to an immovable and self-necessary first principle, as was shown in the body of the Article.**

Aquinas rejects Anselm's "ontological argument," because it proceeds from a mere idea to a real being. He uses only arguments that begin with empirical data. This shows his Aristotelian epistemology: he believed that all our knowledge begins with sense experience, though it is not limited to sense experience. (This has been called "soft empiricism.")

Modern critiques of Aquinas's arguments, such as Hume's and Kant's, usually reject not only these particular arguments but all metaphysical arguments, and even the assumption that causality itself is a universal and objective reality.

## Theological Epistemology: Our Knowledge of God

Aquinas deduces, by reason, a number of attributes of God. E.g., from the premise that He is most unified, or one, or "simple," it follows that (1) He has no composition of potentiality and actuality, or (2) of matter and form, or (3) of substance and accident, or (4) of essence and existence.

(1) He has no composition of act (actuality) and potency (potentiality) because He has no potentiality to change: how could perfection become either better or worse?

(2) He has no matter, for matter has parts outside of other parts.

(3) He has no composition between substance and accidents because in Him there are no accidents. (He is not just a being that happens to be good, He is Goodness.)

(4) And because He is necessary and eternal rather than contingent and in need of a cause, there is no composition in Him between essence and existence: His very essence is existence.

Reason can prove all this about His eternal being. Reason can prove that His being, His goodness, His knowledge, and His power cannot be limited. Reason cannot, however, by itself and without divine revelation, prove what depends not on his necessary nature but on His free choice: e.g., to create a universe, to love and save mankind, or to miraculously intervene in history.

We cannot know God's infinite essence (**what God is**), only (1) **what God is not** ("negative theology") and (2) **what God is like** ("analogical" theology). E.g., (1) we can know that God is not a shark or a man, because these contain limitations. And (2) we can know that God is like creatures, or rather that creatures are like God, because all perfections (truth, goodness, beauty) in them faintly resemble Him, as art resembles the mind of the artist. Analogies are meaningful because they lead in the right direction, even though they do not arrive at their destination, i.e., they do not define what they point to. For instance, God is more like a shark than a rock (since He lives, but not with mortal animal life), more like man than a shark (since He has mind and free will), and more like a good man than a bad man (e.g., a good shepherd, or the loving father of the Prodigal Son).

God is both transcendent to all creatures (point (1) above) and imminent or present to all creatures (point (2)) as Shakespeare is both transcendent to and present to every character and event in His plays.

Attributes that imply imperfections such as passivity and temporality cannot be applied to God at all. It is literally true that God is *not* a beast, an angry man throwing down lightning bolts, or a quantity of energy. Attributes like anger, or sorrow, and actions like shepherding and caring, can be applied to God metaphorically (since they *can* designate human perfections) but not literally (since they imply passivity and limitation). This also applies to metaphors from nature like "rock" or "lion." Attributes like "wise" or "just" or "powerful" can be truly and literally, not metaphorically, attributed to God but only *analogically*, since among us they imply relativity, passivity, and imperfection and because they do not constitute our very essence, as they do in God. Perfections that do not imply any limitations, like being, intelligence, goodness, charity, oneness, freedom, power, and beauty, are literally in God, in a perfect way, and in creatures in imperfect ways. But the difference between their presence in God and their presence in us is so great that we cannot comprehend *what* such perfections as infinite intelligence or charity are in God, only *that* they are in God. (This was Job's lesson about divine justice.) We cannot comprehend them, but we can apprehend them; we can know that they are real.

This is not sufficient for knowledge, but since we *can* know that God is, even though we cannot know *what* He is, it is sufficient for faith, hope, and love. Our love can exceed our knowledge. This is true not only toward God but also toward each other. Aquinas is *not* a rationalist.

## Metaphysics

The most distinctive teaching in Aquinas's metaphysics is the primacy of existence as the supreme actuality and therefore the supreme perfection.

Existence is not simply a brute fact, added to essences, but the fullness of being. Essences are limitations on existence, as the quantity of atoms limit and define the energy of a chemical element, river banks limit and define a river, or the shape of a statue limits and defines the statue.

Essences are only potentialities for existence. Existence is the supreme actuality, that which first of all distinguishes a horse from a unicorn. (Its horn only distinguishes a unicorn's essence from a horse's essence.) All the perfection in a horse comes from its existence, since it is existence that actualizes its essence.

Thus to say that **God is pure being (existence, *esse*, the act "to be")** is *not* to reduce Him to an abstraction—for existence is not an abstraction—but to exalt Him to the supreme perfection—for existence is the supreme perfection, the actuality of all perfections. Existence is *not a fact but an act*. It is the richest term, not the poorest. It includes all perfections because it is the actualization or actuality of them all.

The fact that God is being (existence itself) simultaneously accounts for (1) His total *transcendence* of all beings and (2) His total *imminence* or presence in all beings. For existence both (1) transcends all (finite) essences, as light transcends all colors, or as thought transcends all its objects, and at the same time also (2) actualizes all essences by its presence in them, as light actualizes all colors, or as thought is present to all its objects.

Since (a) existence transcends every contingent being, and since (b) God is existence, therefore (c) God transcends every being.

But since (a) existence is at the heart of every being, as **that which is innermost in each thing and most fundamentally present within all things,** and since (b) God is existence, therefore (c) God is innermost in each thing, present at the heart of every being. The only One who is totally transcendent is also the One who is totally immanent, and both for the same reason: He is the unlimited fullness of existence itself.

Contrast Aquinas's notion of being as existence with (1) Plato's notion of being as Form or Essence, (2) Plotinus' notion of being as something inferior to Unity, or The One, (3) Aristotle's notion of being as substance, (4) Augustine's notion of being as eternity and immutability, and (5) existentialists' notion of being as *human* existence. (See Gilson's *Being and Some Philosophers* on this.) Gilson calls Aquinas's notion of being "the Ultima Thule of metaphysics." Aquinas himself called it **this sublime truth** ("haec sublimas veritas," and ascribed it not to his own philosophizing but to God, who revealed it from the burning bush to Moses in revealing His own eternal name as "I AM WHO AM" (Ex. 3:14). The name tells the nature. God's very name, nature, and essence is being itself.

(It is also *person* ["I"]; Aquinas also says that **person is that which is highest in being**. Thus modern personalism naturally fits as a kind of second story on Aquinas's metaphysical building.)

The simplest way to distinguish God from creatures is to note that God's essence is existence (this is why He needs no cause of His existence), while in all creatures there is a real distinction between their essence (*what* they are) and their existence (*that* they are), so that they need an external cause for their existence, since existence is not internal to their essence. Aquinas inherited this point from the Muslim philosopher Al Kindi (ch. 43) through Avicenna (ch. 46).

Aquinas argues that only one being can be the *total* perfection of actual existence itself, because if there were two, they would have to be different by *some* perfection, thus the other would be less perfect.

Aquinas says that all created beings are composed of essence and existence, which is the ultimate level of potentiality-actuality composition. Essences are only potential to existence. Humanness and horseness do not exist by themselves, as Plato believed, but these essences come into being only when humans or horses are given actual existence; and the essence exists only in those humans or horses.

Existence both divides all beings (many beings having the same essence—e.g., many horses—can exist) and also unites all beings, since it is what is common to all beings. Stones, flowers, dogs, men, and angels all exist. A prisoner in solitary confinement, deprived of all human, animal, and plant communities, can still rejoice in the community of existents by feeling an existing stone. He has something that unites him with it: existence. Yet it is a real *other*.

A second level of metaphysical composition, besides essence and existence, is substance and accident, as in Aristotle. This explains how a being can change and yet remain itself. (See ch. 25, page 128.)

A third level of composition is matter and form, also as in Aristotle. Matter is the metaphysical principle of individuation, like a Xerox machine replicating the same text (form) on different pieces of matter (paper). This explains how there can be many beings in the same species (form), e.g., many horses. (Accidental forms also distinguish them, but only if matter has done so first. Two Xeroxed copies of a book may differ by one having a water droplet on it, but they are first made to be two by two different pieces of paper in the copy machine.)

## Cosmology

(1) The most important fact about the universe for Aquinas is that it has been created. What the Greeks called "the cosmos" (the ordered whole of things, including men and gods) Jews, Christians, and Muslims called "the creation." It was relative to God, not gods relative to it, as in ancient paganism.

To create is to make something from nothing—not from no efficient or final or formal cause but from no material cause, from no pre-existing material. This could be done by none of the pagan gods; thus their "creation stories" are not literally creation stories at all but formation stories. The pagan gods impose pre-existing forms on pre-existing matter. The God of the Bible creates matter itself. He can do this only because one can give only what one already has or is, and only this God is existence itself, therefore only this God can give existence, which is what "creating" means.

(2) God must have created freely, not necessarily (as Plotinus's "One" necessarily emanates). His motive could only have been pure charity, the desire to give, not to get, to share His perfection with other beings for their sake, not His.

Yet, though it was a free choice of His will, the act of creation was fitting, and reasonable, and in accordance with His nature as creative, free, and generous.

(3) Everything in the creation resembles some perfection in the Creator, beginning with its "ontological generosity" (Maritain's term), its tendency to communicate itself to other beings. Everything is related to everything; even an electron makes a difference to other particles.

The ultimate source of this is not knowable except by divine revelation; it is the nature of God as a Trinity of Persons eternally giving themselves to each other. ("God IS love.") What God did in creating a universe of time outside Himself expressed and fit with what He does eternally within Himself.

(4) All created being is less than absolutely perfect, even though it can be relatively perfect in its kind, e.g., a perfect sunset or a perfect 300 bowling score. Therefore physical evils (defects) are possible. The lack of absolute perfection makes possible the lack of relative perfection. This lack of relative perfection does not mean finitude; a perfect rose is finite, not infinite. But a dirty rose or a diseased rose is an imperfect rose.

For "the perfection of the universe" as a whole, Aquinas argues, God uses physical evils, as an artist uses darkness in one part of a painting for the greater glory of the light in another part, and for the greater beauty of the whole painting.

Evil is a not a being but a lack; but it is a real lack. It is not an entity, a substance, a thing; it is the lack of some perfection in a being that should have it—e.g., blindness, pain, or disease. **Ens est bonum;** all being is ontologically good. (Cf. Augustine on this, ch. 36, p. 31.)

The worst kind of evil is moral evil, which comes from man's free choice, not God's creation. **Sin is worse than pain**, Aquinas says. (Do you agree? Why or why not?)

God is not the cause of either kind of actual evil, physical or moral, though He is the cause of the possibility of both, in (1) creating finite things, thus making possible physical evils, and in (2) creating man with free will.

(5) Aristotle believed that the universe was eternal and uncreated (thus that time past was infinite) and that this could be proved. Bonaventure believed that the universe was created and that past time was finite, and that this could be proved, since an infinite number of days or moments cannot be crossed or traversed, so that if time past were infinite, we never could have reached today. Aquinas believed that the universe was created and that time past was finite but that this could not be proved by reason alone, but only known by divine revelation. For God *could* have created a universe eternally dependent on Him if He had willed to, and what depends on God's free will cannot be proved by necessary reasons. (Today the finitude of past time has been proved by physical science.)

(6) Like all pre-moderns, Aquinas saw the universe as a hierarchy, a "great chain of being." The most perfect of all creatures are angels, who are pure spirits of far greater intelligence and power than men. He believed there was a strong probable argument for their existence from natural reason, since if they did not exist there would be a great gap in the chain of being between man and God; and there are no gaps "downward": all possible levels of animals, plants, and minerals exist. It is a kind of argument from the analogy with animals.

Matter individuates different beings in the same species. But angels are pure spirits, without matter. They are individualized not by matter but by form alone. Therefore each angel is a different form, or essence, or species. Michael and Gabriel are different not like Laddie and Lassie but like Dog and Cat.

Because Aquinas's philosophy, unlike Aristotle's, had an essence-existence composition as well as a matter-form composition, he could distinguish angels from both men and God. Though they have no matter (no matter-form composition) to distinguish them from God, they have the essence-existence distinction, which God does not have. God alone is pure actuality; even angels are potential to existence, and must be created (given existence).

## Anthropology

(1) Although matter is the first principle of individuation metaphysically, it does not adequately account for individuality in human personalities. Matter only makes individuality possible; in itself it is only potentiality, which cannot account for any actual perfection. That comes from actual being (i.e., existence—remember, existence for Aquinas is an act, not just a fact).

(2) Aquinas follows Aristotle's hylomorphism (form-and-matter) regarding man. He is neither a materialist (like Democritus) nor a spiritualist (like Shankara) nor a dualist (like Descartes, ch. 58, who sees soul and body as two substances, one spiritual and one material). He defines man as a single substance composed of matter (the body) and form (the soul). These are not two entities or substances but two mutually relative dimensions of the one substance, man, somewhat as the words and the meaning of a book are the material and spiritual dimensions of the book. **The soul is the form of the body** and the body is the matter for the soul.

(3) The basic meaning of "soul" in Aquinas, as in Aristotle, is **the first principle** (source) **of life, movement, and growth in a living being**. The soul is what leaves the body of a man, a cow, or a tulip when it dies. In this sense of "soul" animals and even plants have souls too. But only man has a rational soul.

(4) Some of Aquinas's contemporaries taught that man had three souls. But Aquinas holds that man's single soul has three kinds of powers: vegetative, sensitive (animal), and rational (distinctively human) powers. It is the same soul that keeps the body alive and that thinks and chooses. This is why the body is holy: because the source of the body's biological life is an immortal spirit made in God's image and possessing freedom and moral responsibility.

(5) Unlike plant and animal souls, man's soul is immortal because it is not merely the form of the body but also a substance with its own act of existence called "subsistence," which it gives to the body. (After all, a man has a single act of existence, not two.) A soul without a body, though it can exist, is an incomplete man and an incomplete substance; after death a new "resurrection" body is necessary to complete its humanity.

(6) Another argument for the soul's immortality is our innate longing for it. **Nature makes nothing in vain**, including desires. As the poet Browning put it, "a man's reach must exceed his grasp, or what's a Heaven for?"

(7) Still another argument is the fact that the soul has a work (abstract intellectual understanding) that transcends the work of the body; and an immaterial act like this can

be performed only by an immaterial being. Therefore the soul is immaterial, and material death cannot kill it.

(8) Thus Aquinas fits together (1) the Aristotelian hylomorphic unity (what psychologists today call "the psychosomatic unity") and (2) the soul's substantiality and continued existence after the body dies. The soul is both a substance (not *merely* the form of the body) *and* the form of the body. This may be a tricky and uneasy synthesis, like Augustine's synthesis of free will and predestination, but the two contrasting parts of the data are both evident (rather like light being both wave and particle). Denying half the data would be a far worse error than a not wholly satisfactory explanation of how the two halves are logically compatible.

(9) Augustine and his more Platonic followers did not think the soul was the form of the body because they thought a soul should not lower itself, so to speak, to serve a lesser thing. Aquinas's answer is that it is the body that serves the soul, since we need the senses and sense experience in order to know anything, as we need desires in order for the will to judge and order them morally. To do its work as mind and will, the soul needs the body's perceptions and instinctive desires to use as matter or raw material. The body is the stone and glass of the cathedral that is man.

## Epistemology

(1) Here too Aquinas synthesizes Platonic-Augustinian and Aristotelian insights, especially (a) Augustine's notion of "divine illumination" and the intellect's receptivity to forms or essences through this illumination and (b) Aristotle's notion of the intellect actively abstracting forms from matter. He accepts Aristotle's abstractionism as the proximate or immediate cause of our knowledge, and Augustine's illuminationism as its ultimate cause.

The object of purely intellectual understanding is a (Platonic) Idea (essence), and Aquinas says an Idea exists in three places: ***ante rem*** (before the thing) in the Mind of God as the design or model for a created thing; ***in re*** (in the thing) as its form; and ***post rem*** (after the thing) in our minds after we abstract this form from the thing's matter. So you might call him one-third a Platonist and two-thirds an Aristotelian. The created material world (*in re*) is the means by which God communicates His Ideas (*ante rem*) to our minds (*post rem*). So human science is the reading of divine art.

(2) Aquinas summarized the history of epistemology under three options.

(a) The first is that of some of the Presocratics, who deduced the epistemological conclusion of skepticism from their metaphysical premise of materialism (for if reality is limited to changing things and knowledge is limited to sensation, the objects of knowledge are never stable but always changing).

(b) The second is that of Plato, who sharply distinguished forms (Ideas) from matter metaphysically, the soul from the body anthropologically, and reason from the senses epistemologically. This overcame skepticism but at the price of separating what is really together.

(c) The third and best option is Aristotle's hylomorphic synthesis of form and matter, soul and body, reason and senses.

(3) Avicenna and Averroes interpreted Aristotle to mean that the intellect by which we actively abstract forms from matter is a single entity in which all men participate. Aquinas argued, against this, that we are each aware of our individual ability to abstract and to understand what we abstract.

(4) Understanding the essence, form, nature, or Idea of a thing and abstracting it from material individuals must be simultaneous. For if abstraction *precedes* understanding, how can we understand what to abstract? And if understanding precedes abstraction, we do not need abstraction in order to understand.

(5) Aquinas is thus, like Aristotle, a "soft empiricist": he believes that human knowledge begins in sensation, but does not end in it. The mind has no innate ideas that it can simply remember, as Plato thought, but is like a **tabula rasa** ("blank tablet"), as Aristotle taught. But the intellect as active (the "agent intellect") can abstract forms from matter, and the intellect as passive can receive and understand them. ("Receptive" is a better translation than "passive," for catching a ball is as much an act as throwing it.)

(6) Following Aristotle, Aquinas distinguishes three acts of the mind, or rational acts, which distinguish humans from animals: (a) conception, or understanding, the object of which is an essence (e.g., "mortal"); (b) judgment, the object of which is existence (e.g., "Man *is* mortal"); and (c) reasoning, the object of which is a cause, real or logical (e.g., "Man is mortal and Socrates is a man, *therefore* Socrates is mortal").

(7) Truth exists in judgments, which join two concepts (e.g., "Man is mortal"), not in a mere single concept (like "mortal"). Reasoning moves from some truths (the premises) to another truth (the conclusion).

(8) Truth also exists in things, as well as minds, because truth is **adequatio intellectus et rei**, the match between the mind and real things. Intellectual truth is the human mind's conformity to things (the universe), and ontological truth is the universe's conformity to the divine Mind that designed and created it.

(9) This is not a "correspondence theory of truth," however, as in classical modern epistemology (Descartes and Locke), but an identity theory. If our thoughts merely

corresponded to things, as an image or picture corresponded to the thing it was an image or picture of, we would directly know only the image, not the thing, in which case we could never be sure which images corresponded and which did not. Instead, it is the very same identical form which exists both in the thing (e.g., treeness in a tree) and in the mind that knows the tree. If it were not the same form, the knowledge would not be true.

(10) Concepts are not the objects of the mind, for Aquinas, as they are for Descartes and Locke; real things are. Concepts (which are abstracted from sense images or "phantasms") are the *means* ("quo") of knowing, not the objects ("quod") known. (Cf. ST I, 85, 2.) If they were the objects known, all sciences would be divisions of psychology, i.e., their objects would be what is in the soul, not what is outside it; and we could never know which ones corresponded to real things, so skepticism would result.

(11) Theoretical judgments are about what is; practical judgments are about what ought to be, what ought to be done or made. Practical judgments are not about present facts but desired goods, and their truth consists in the intellect's conformity with right desire, not with being. In morality the intellect's standard and rule is the will's desire for the true good, especially the good of human nature. Thus, human nature is the proximate standard for morality.

## Ethics

(1) Thus we have a "**natural law** morality." Moral law is based on human nature, its true goods and ends and needs. Good acts perfect our human nature; evil acts harm it.

Three levels of natural law are distinguished: (a) its primary precept, which is to **do good and avoid evil**, (b) its immediate secondary precepts like "do not kill, steal, lie, or commit adultery," and (c) its derivative or tertiary precepts like "restore stolen property, do not abort, and parents should sacrifice for their children." All are binding, but there are different degrees of subjective knowing of them, since premises are more clearly known than conclusions and (a) is the premise for (b) and (b) for (c). No one can doubt (a), very few people doubt (b), and significantly more people doubt (c). But **the natural law can never be completely abolished from the heart of man, though it can be obscured by disordered passions**.

(2) This "natural law" is distinguished from **eternal law**, which is God's mind and will providentially planning what is good for His creation. The natural law is a participation in or expression of the eternal law.

(3) The natural law is also distinguished from "**human law**" (called "positive law" in modern philosophy because it is "posited" by human wills). Human law is invented and willed by man and thus differs somewhat from one time, place, and community to

another; and these differences are proper, as long as they do not contradict the natural law.

Human law is binding, but not absolutely. Obedience is always the default position, so to speak—Aquinas is more "conservative" than "progressive"—but natural law moralists like Aquinas can have moral justification for civil disobedience and even revolution in extreme cases because of their belief in a higher law than human law. Moral relativists, who do not believe in any "higher law," do not have this justification for rebellion; thus their morality logically ought to be more "conservative" toward human laws than Aquinas's.

(4) A fourth kind of law, which Aquinas calls "**divine law**," is God's revealed will for one people, time, or place, such as the Jewish ceremonial laws. Unlike both eternal law and natural law, divine law, like human law, is contingent and changeable, though divine law is changeable only by God while human law is changeable by man.

(5) The common essence of all law is **an ordinance** (deliberate ordering) **of reason for the common good, made by the one who has the care of the community, and promulgated.** Law is made by *reason*, not mere will; by definition it is not arbitrary.

(6) The two guides to the good life are laws, which direct us from without, and virtues, which direct us from within. Virtues are good habits.

There are (a) five "intellectual virtues," distinguished by Aristotle:

(1) contemplative "science," whose object is necessary truth,

(2) practical "art," whose object is contingent things,

(3) "practical wisdom," deliberating about human goods,

(4) "intuitive reason," the knowledge of first principles, and

(5) "theoretical wisdom," the union of (1) and (4);

(b) there are also "the four cardinal moral virtues" of prudence (practical wisdom), fortitude (courage), temperance (self-control) and justice, distinguished by Plato and

(c) finally, there are "the three theological virtues" of faith, hope, and charity, distinguished by scripture.

(7) The most distinctive feature of Aquinas's ethics is its metaphysical basis. Everything in the universe is restless with activity and change, whether physical, biological, or psychological. The ultimate reason for this dynamism is found in their Creator, who is the dynamic act of be-ing (existing, *esse*). This "first act" always results in the "second act" or activity: *operatio sequitur esse,* "operating follows existing." All creatures act and change because they are ordered to the infinitely perfect God as their ultimate end and good: acorns grow into oak trees ultimately because mature oaks have in them more of what God is—perfection, ontological goodness. Man too fits into this cosmic context, as Augustine famously said: "Thou hast made us for Thyself, and (this is why) our hearts are restless until they rest in Thee."

(8) In man this striving is both conscious and free, both rational and moral. Human free will is "rational appetite." Animal desire is sensory appetite. Plant growth is an "inclination' from within. Physical movement is an "inclination" from without that we call gravity. (Gravity is the lowest form of love. Dante called it "the love that moves the sun and other stars.")

(9) Aquinas's argument for free will is very simple and practical: **man has free will, otherwise all praise, blame, counseling, commanding, rewarding and punishing are in vain** (meaningless)**.** We do not do any of these things to machines. When the Coke machine takes our money without delivering the Coke, we do not send it to confession.

We have free will because we do not have a clear, face-to-face vision of God in this life, and thus we can choose many different goals, many different candidates for happiness, and many different means to that end. In Heaven alone will the joy of the "beatific vision" make temptation to sin impossible. We will then have the higher freedom of what Augustine calls "*libertas*" (liberty) instead of the lower freedom of indetermination of will, which requires deliberation and choice ("*liberum arbitrium*").

(10) Insofar as man attains his natural end and good, he experiences joy. **No man can live without joy; that is why one deprived of true spiritual joys will go over to carnal pleasures.**

(11) Joy is the will's response to present good. Desire is the will's response to absent good. But it must be the intellect that unites us with the supreme good; union with God is an act of the intellect "the beatific *vision*," though an act of the will is both its cause (choice) and its effect (enjoyment). The efficient *cause* of man's union with God is his will freely desiring, loving and choosing it (and, of course, divine grace is the very first cause of the whole process); and the *effect* of this union is the will's joy, or rejoicing in it; but *the union itself* consists in the intellect *knowing* God (the "beatific vision"). (Cf. Jn 17:3.) This "knowing" is not abstract but personal and concrete: its object is not a proposition but a Person. The will is the power that brings us to God but the mind is the glue that unites us to Him.

(12) That is one reason why Aquinas believes the intellect is in itself superior to the will. Another reason is that it is authoritative: it is the navigator, whose charts must be obeyed by the captain (the will) if the ship is to attain its true goal.

Yet the captain also rules the navigator. Reason and will rule and depend on each other in different ways, for knowing is the formal and final cause of willing, while willing is the efficient cause of knowing (the "will to know").

Aquinas says that **it is better to love God than to know God** because love draws the lover into the beloved, conforms the lover to the beloved, while knowing does the opposite: it conforms the knowledge to the knower in the sense that it grasps only those dimensions of its object that it is capable of receiving; and in this life the human mind is radically limited in its ability to know God, while there is no limit set on our love of God.

Because of the principle above, it is better to know than love what is inferior to us but better to love than know what is superior to us. When we know a diamond, we lift the diamond up into our own mental life, which is superior to it. When we love a diamond, we lower ourselves down to its level, letting it fill our heart. But when we love God, we move up toward His level, while when we know Him we lower Him (i.e., whatever we can know of Him) down to our level. That is why it is better to love God than to know God but better to know a diamond than to love it.

Thus Aquinas is neither simply an intellectualist nor simply a voluntarist.

(13) Aquinas as a Christian knew that merely natural, rational virtue is incomplete. Reason alone can tell us, as it told pagans like Plato and Aristotle, that our supreme happiness lies in union with God; and it can show us our natural desire for God; but it cannot tell us how to attain this desire. Only God's supernatural grace and love, revealed in history (the Incarnation) and accepted by faith, can meet and fulfill our deepest natural longing. Bottom line: without Christ we are doomed to ultimate pessimism and frustration. Ultimately, Aquinas's ethics is a detailing, or "unpackaging," or completion, of Augustine's "restless heart." He synthesizes not only Augustine and Aristotle, theology and philosophy, the Bible and the Greeks, soul and body, reason and senses, intellect and will, faith and reason, natural and supernatural, but even God and man, in Christ. His philosophy is the ultimate "both-and" instead of "either-or."

What a tragedy that there was no Aquinas among Islamic philosophers to mediate between the "liberal" naturalist and rationalist heretics like Averroes and the supernaturalist but irrationalist voluntarist fundamentalists like the Ash'arites.

### Selected Bibliography

1. G. K. Chesterton, *St. Thomas Aquinas, the Dumb Ox*
2. Etienne Gilson,
    a. *The Christian Philosophy of St. Thomas Aquinas*
    b. *The Elements of Christian Philosophy*
    c. *Thomist Realism*
    d. *Moral Values and the Moral Life*
    e. *Being and Some Philosophers*
3. Jacques Maritain,
    a. *The Degrees of Knowledge*
    b. *An Introduction to Philosophy*
    c. *Art and Scholasticism*
    d. *Scholasticism and Politics*
    e. *A Preface to Metaphysics*
    f. *Existence and the Existent*

4. Ralph McInerny: *First Glance at Thomas Aquinas: A Handbook for Peeping Thomists*

5. W. Norris Clarke, S.J.,

    a. *The One and the Many* (Thomas's metaphysics)

    b. *Person and Being* (why metaphysical Thomism and modern personalism need each other)

    c. *The Philosophical Approaches to God*

    d. *Explorations in Metaphysics*

6. Peter Kreeft, ed., *Summa of the Summa* (Aquinas's important philosophical passages edited and explained); *Practical Theology* (Aquinas's "existential" moral and religious passages commented on)

7. Louis de Wohl, *The Quiet Light* (novel)

8. Josef Pieper,

    a. ed., *The Human Wisdom of St. Thomas*

    b. *The Silence of St. Thomas*

    c. *Guide to Thomas Aquinas*

9. Kenneth Gallagher, *The Philosophy of Knowledge*

10. Frederick Wilhelmsen, *Man's Knowledge of Reality*

# 51. Duns Scotus (1266–1308)

His name was John Duns. Because he was born in Scotland he was called "Scotus," or "the Scot." Because after his death his disciples sometimes "settled" arguments merely by quoting his authority, his opponents replied "You're a dunsman," which was shortened to "You're a dunce," which is the source of that insulting word. He joined the Franciscans, studied at Oxford and Paris, and later taught at both places. He died at only 42. According to some sources, he fell into a coma, was wrongly believed dead, and was buried alive. When his tomb was opened his body was found outside his coffin, with his hands bloodied from trying to escape. (Life was not easy in those days. Neither was death.)

## The Salient Point: the "Corrective" to Rationalism

All philosophers are part of a story, "the great conversation" that is the history of philosophy. All of them confront problems, difficulties, dangers, or errors that are peculiar to their time: e.g., in ancient philosophy, Parmenides vs. Heraclitus, Socrates vs. the Sophists, and Stoics vs. Epicureans; in medieval philosophy, Bonaventure and the Augustinians vs. the naturalism and rationalism of Aristotle, Averroes, Siger of Brabant, and the "double truth" theory; and in modern philosophy, the Empiricism of Locke and Hume vs. the Rationalism of Descartes; and, later, the Existentialists vs. the Rationalists, Pascal vs. Descartes, Kierkegaard vs. Hegel. Very occasionally a philosopher like Aristotle, Aquinas, or Kant comes along whose strategy is to synthesize opposite insights rather than opposing them to each other. Most philosophers are "correctives" to what they view as erroneous extremes about some issue. And one common issue in all the examples above is the extent of the power of human reason.

The philosophy against which Scotus is reacting or correcting is often labeled "Latin Averroism" by historians. Centuries before, the Muslim philosopher Averroes had defended Aristotle's ideal of a purely natural, rational philosophy with no need for, reliance on, or synthesis with, divine revelation. Instead of simply denying divine revelation, some Christians like Siger of Brabant, following Averroes, taught a "double truth" theory: that a proposition could be philosophically true and theologically false at the same time—in other words, that truth is not single and objective but a matter of personal perspective. Those who taught this always implied that the superior perspective was philosophy, not religion. Religion, like pagan mythology, was for them the best that ordinary minds could do, but philosophers could rise above this. Correlative to this rationalism for man there was a rationalism for God, so to speak: God always acted by rational necessity, not by unpredictable free choice.

Duns Scotus's main "corrective" to this rationalism is his emphasis on freedom and the will. This opposed the rationalism and necessitarianism (or fatalism) of the Greeks (both Plato and Aristotle), both in man and in God. Scotus is often classified as a voluntarist. This is overly simplistic, but he is closer to a voluntarist than an intellectualist or rationalist.

Scotus emphasizes human reason's *intrinsic* limitations. Anselm and Bonaventure also emphasized reason's relative inferiority to faith, but both had very optimistic views of the extent of reason's power to know the mysteries of the Faith, which extended to rationally demonstrating even the Trinity and the Incarnation, for Anselm, or at least that the universe was created in time and is not eternal, for Bonaventure. Though Scotus, like all major medieval philosophers, shared the same faith as Aquinas, Anselm, and Bonaventure, he was less optimistic about the extent of its synthesis with philosophical reason, and about the power of natural reason especially concerning our knowledge of God.

He did not go so far as some other Franciscans and Augustinians of his time did. They claimed that we need a supernatural act of God to overcome skepticism and to have any certain knowledge at all. Scotus replied we could know with certainty by reason alone (1) self-evident first principles like the law of non-contradiction, (2) immediate empirical facts (e.g., "eclipses happen"), and (3) our own interior acts of knowing and loving that are immediately present to our consciousness.

Yet like Bonaventure, Scotus argues that philosophers like Aristotle, who relied on natural reason alone, inevitably fell into error because of their ignorance of Original Sin and the epistemic consequences of the Fall. Scotus maintained that even man's present dependence on sense experience for rational knowledge is not his created and intended state but a result of the Fall. (This is one of the many issues on which he disagreed with Aquinas.)

### Scotus's Alternative to Thomistic Metaphysics

The three most distinctive Scotist doctrines in metaphysics, in distinction from Thomist alternatives, are (1) the denial of the real distinction between essence and existence, (2) the doctrine that being is univocal, not analogical; and (3) the notion of "thisness" (*hecceitas*) as the principle of individuation.

The connection among these three theses is as follows.

(1) Scotus argues against the real distinction between essence and existence from the premise that (a) human reason cannot reach the act of existence itself, and also from the premise that (b) existents are so radically distinct from each other that they have no intelligible unity. Scotus claimed that essence and existence were identical not only in God but in themselves, and called existence merely a mode of essence, making existence relative to essence rather than essence relative to existence (as the potentiality for existence) as Aquinas had taught.

(2) So the only way metaphysics can have a unified object (being) is, not to claim

that its object is existence (*esse*), as Aquinas does, but to consider being as abstracted from and indifferent to either universality or individuality (e.g., either horseness or this existing horse), and thus as univocal (having one and only one meaning) rather than analogical (having a range of related meanings).

(3) If an essence (e.g., horseness) were of itself universal, he argues, then no individuals (horses) could exist; and if it were of itself individual, then no universal species could exist, but only one concrete horse. Thus, what individuates beings is neither form nor matter but *hecceitas,* "thisness," the actuality that restricts a species' form to this one singular individual. Perhaps the best "take" on this very abstract concept would be to see it simply as the fact of individuality or singularity itself. It functions in the same way for Scotus as the act of existing (*esse*) functions for Aquinas, as the ultimate reality in a being, that accounts for the actuality of everything else in it. For Scotus, *hecceitas* accounts also for the individuality of a being's *esse*; for Aquinas, *esse* accounts also for the individuality of a being's *hecceitas*.

Scotus's *hecceitas* ("thisness") was a favorite notion of the poet Gerard Manly Hopkins, S.J. He saw it as the unique individuality of a concrete thing in nature that the poet intuits, and called it "inscape."

### Scotus's Proof for the Existence of God

Scotus accepted the premises and the logic of Aristotle's arguments for the existence of God but criticized the thinness of their conclusion. They proved merely some first, unmoved mover of matter in time, not an absolutely unique Infinite Being. In other words, Aristotle's proofs worked, but what they proved hardly deserved to be called "God."

All arguments for God's existence have the same conclusion, but differ in their premises. Aquinas chose concrete empirical premises like causality and motion, but Scotus chose the much more abstract metaphysical premise that *some being is producible* (able to be produced, possible to come into existence).

Since this is only a truth about possible being, not actually existing being, his argument must make a transition from possibility to actuality. He does this by arguing that if this being (God) did not actually exist, it would be impossible. And since it has already been admitted to be possible, it must therefore be actually existent.

Why would it be impossible if it did not actually exist? Because we are talking about a being that is the *first, uncaused* cause, and thus nothing else could possibly cause it to be, or account for its existence, since there can be nothing prior to the absolutely First. So if it did not exist, it could not be caused to exist and would thus be impossible. So the only reason God (an un-caused First Cause) is possible is that He is actual.

(The proof assumes what Leibnitz would later formulate as the Principle of Sufficient Reason: that everything that exists must have a reason sufficient to account for its existence. Creatures' sufficient reason for existing is extrinsic to them, in their Creator; God's sufficient reason for existing is intrinsic to Himself, in His own essence.)

That argument considered efficient causes. Scotus has similar arguments about final and formal causes, which prove that it is also necessary to posit an absolutely Last End or primary final cause in order to account for relative ends, and a Being whose essence or form is absolutely perfect in order to account for relative perfections of form.

A second argument begins not with an attribute relative to creatures, namely causality, but with an attribute intrinsic to God Himself, unique to God Himself, and according to Scotus the most perfect idea of God that we can form by reason in this life, namely *infinity*. The argument is essentially that an infinite being is possible, therefore it exists. If it did not exist, it would be impossible. For no *other* reason, outside itself, could possibly be given for its possibility.

Scotus claims here to have altered and improved the argument of Anselm, by centering on Anselm's point that it is self-contradictory to conceive of God as nonexistent.

Scotus argues for God's infinity this way: an absolutely first, un-caused cause, efficient, final or formal, is not limited, and therefore is infinite, because to be limited by something is to be caused by that something.

Also, this First Cause must be infinite because, being perfect, it knows everything knowable; but "everything knowable" is infinite because there is no limit to the number of possible beings that are intelligible. Since infinite intelligence is required to know infinite intelligible objects, God's intelligence must be infinite.

A parallel argument proves that God's *goodness* is infinite. Our will by nature desires a supreme, absolute, first, and therefore infinite good. This would be impossible if such a good was an impossible and therefore nonexistent being. (It is psychologically impossible to desire what is metaphysically and logically impossible to exist, e.g., a being that is both free and unfree, or infinite and non-infinite, at the same time and in the same way.) Therefore there must be an infinitely good Being. When considering the objects of the human mind and the will, as well as when considering the order of being itself, Scotus deduces actuality from possibility.

## Our Knowledge of God

Aquinas taught that (1) we do not know *what* God is, only *that* He is, and that (2) we know God by negation (what God is not) and (3) by analogy (what God is like, or rather what is like God). Scotus criticized all three of these points, as follows.

(1) We cannot know that God exists without knowing *what* this thing that exists is. To say merely that "x exists" is to say nothing.

(2) Negative knowledge is worthless unless based on positive knowledge: if we know merely that God is not a stone, we cannot distinguish Him from nothingness, since nothingness is also not a stone.

(3) Analogy is worthless because only univocal concepts can come from abstraction,

and our notion of being comes only by abstraction. (Aquinas denies the premise of this argument, as well as the premises of the first two.)

Having weakened Thomistic reason this much, the only way remaining for Scotus to know God is by divine revelation; this is how he says we know God's attributes such as omnipotence, omnipresence, justice, and mercy.

### Created Being

"Why is there anything rather than nothing?" Only God is necessary being; all other being is contingent (it does not have to be). Why then does it exist? Only the will of God can cause anything other than God to exist.

Scotus was keenly aware of the metaphysical difference between the Greek view that the universe was eternal and necessary and the Biblical doctrine of God's free creation of the universe. The universe was now contingent, not necessary, in every detail, down to its very existence. For the Greeks (and the Latin Averroists who followed them) it was only *matter* that made things contingent; forms were necessary and eternal, whether Platonically (as separately existing Ideas) or Aristotelianly (even for Aristotle, species were eternal, though individuals were not). For Christians, everything except God was contingent on God's free will and choice to create this universe rather than none or rather than any one of the infinite number of alternative logically possible universes (e.g., one without horses, or with dragons, or with orange, two-headed silicon-based animals, or even with a different kind of matter).

All Jews and Christians believe that the universe is contingent upon God's free creation of it, but Scotus drew more radical and negative (skeptical) consequences from this doctrine than previous philosophers had done.

### Anthropology

Here too Scotus's tendency is to demote or weaken the claims made for human reason not only by Aristotle but also by Aquinas. Contrary to Aquinas, Scotus maintains that only faith in divine revelation, and not rational philosophy, can know that the soul has been directly created by God, that it is immaterial, or that it is immortal.

Scotus argues for the absolute primacy of the will in man by saying that we know only because we will to know, so the will commands the intellect. It is the efficient cause of the intellect's acts. Aquinas agreed with this point but balanced it by the primacy of the intellect in formal and final causality. Scotus replied that this is merely an accidental or occasional cause of willing.

With regard to God, Scotus is also something of a voluntarist: not that the divine will commands or ignores the divine intellect within the divine being, but that it is only God's will that chooses among many logically possible essences (and universes, or groups of compossible essences) to create beings outside the divine being.

## Morality

And with regard to morality, Scotus regards only the first three of the Ten Commandments are eternal, necessary and unchangeable truths of the natural law; the other seven, which concern our relations to our neighbors, could have been different had God willed it. God is necessarily our final end (and the first three Commandments regulate that); but God could have willed different temporal means to that end, thus He could have changed the last seven commandments if He had wanted to. God can therefore sometimes make exceptions to them; for example, He allowed the Jews to steal from the Egyptians and commanded Abraham to murder his son Isaac.

Scotus argues that God's own essence is the only necessary object of His will; therefore there is no reason for God's choice to will any universe, or this universe, or this code of morality for human life in this universe. Euthyphro rather than Socrates was right: God does not will an action because it is good, it is good only because God wills it.

These seven commandments are not arbitrary, however, but proper and right; but they are not absolute and unchangeable necessities, just as the universe is not. Scotus applies the same radical contingency to the human part of morality that he applies to the universe. It was left to Ockham to follow Euthyphro and the Ash'arites in making *all* of morality dependent on God's will alone.

# 52. William of Ockham (1288–1348)

## His Era

Thomists usually claim that medieval philosophy in general and Thomism in particular was the mountaintop of the history of philosophy as well as theology, reached by centuries of climbing. If so, why has the slope been downward rather than upward ever since? If the main line of post-Thomistic philosophy has been a series of errors, right up to the present, what is the primary cause of this? Why have all the modern philosophies, even when they included important positive contributions, been mixed with negations and errors?

Even non-Thomists usually agree that Thomas was the peak of *medieval* philosophy, as Aristotle was the peak of ancient Greek philosophy, and that subsequent centuries, at least for almost 500 years, until Descartes, constituted a decline, which necessitated a new beginning with Descartes. Who and what was the villain of this story of decline?

To these questions the answer is William of Ockham and Nominalism.

Ockham was born in England (in Ockham, Surrey). He became a Franciscan and studied and taught at both Oxford and Paris. He was personally abrasive and polemical. He was accused of heresy at the papal court in Avignon in 1324 but was not condemned, though he was later excommunicated for having been involved, together with the General Minister of the Franciscan Order, in political machinations against the temporal power of the Pope. Both had to flee for their lives to the protection of Emperor Ludwig of Bavaria, who had similar anti-papal ambitions. Ockham spent the rest of his life writing tracts against the Pope's political claims.

Compared with the thirteenth century, the fourteenth was one of disintegration, decline, and crisis in every area. The power of the Church suffered severe shocks, including the "Babylonian captivity of the papacy," when the Pope was kidnapped and forced to move to Avignon, France, and to live dependent on the French king. This was followed by the Great Schism, with three different men claiming to be the rightful pope. New heresies arose (Wycliffe and Hus, sort of proto-Protestants) that were more popular and lasting than any before.[*]

---

[*] Classic Dominican joke: What's the difference between the Jesuits and the Dominicans? Answer: The Jesuits were founded to combat the Protestant heresy in the sixteenth century; the Dominicans were founded to combat the Albigensian heresy in the twelfth century. How many Albigensians do you know?

Many rival nationalisms arose, shattering the dream of a unified Christendom. Idealism declined; pessimism, world-weariness, and cynicism increased. The Black Death killed a third of the population of Europe, including Ockham himself. It was like the second coming of the decline and fall of Rome, an economic, political, and social disaster that was almost the equivalent of a nuclear winter.

But unlike the fall of Rome, this crisis did not have an Augustine to arise and reply to it. Philosophy shared the decline and divisions of the century. Disciples of Thomas, Scotus, and Ockham bitterly attacked each other rather than sharing and synthesizing insights as Aquinas had done. The only philosophy that made gains was skepticism. Human reason, like man himself, came to distrust itself more and more. The marriage of faith and reason, theology and philosophy, the supernatural and the natural, had been the central enterprise of Christian philosophy from the beginning (Justin Martyr) through Aquinas. Now came the shock of divorce, a divorce that most centrally defined the philosophical difference between the medieval and modern eras.

## Reason & Faith, Philosophy & Theology

Aquinas had defended theology as a rational science, in fact "the queen of the sciences." Ockham denies that it is a science at all, and says it rests wholly on faith and not at all on reason. Its purpose is not the knowledge of objective truth but merely personal salvation, eternal happiness; it is practical, not theoretical. Ockham reduced the rational understanding of the Faith to a bare minimum.

Centuries later Galileo famously said to the bishops who criticized his theories, "You tell me how to go to Heaven, I'll tell you how the heavens go." Galileo's point was to *distinguish* theology (rightly) from *natural science*; Ockham's was to *separate* it (wrongly) from *philosophy*. But these two things were more closely connected than we probably expect, because (a) Ockham thought that every mental distinction had to be founded on a real separation (he was arguing against abstraction), and because (b) until modern times, the natural sciences were not sharply distinguished from philosophy.

This dualist, separationist, or isolationist point of view about the relation between faith and reason has become the default position of our present Western culture, and Ockham is its primary origin. Already in the fourteenth century it was so self-consciously and radically new that it (and the Nominalism that was its source, by radically reducing reason) was called "the modern way" (*via moderna),* compared with the traditional position of the *via antiqua* ("old way"), i.e., all of the history of Christian philosophy up until then, culminating in Aquinas and Scotus.

Ockham did not doubt or deny the Faith, nor did he believe it logically contradicted reason. He was quite secure in what he believed, but he did not claim to *know* it (i.e., understand it, or to be certain of it intellectually).

The source of this divorce between faith and reason was not a demoting of faith but of reason. For one thing, Ockham taught that "**every science . . . is concerned only with**

**propositions as with objects known, for only propositions are known.**" Reason, as distinct from sensation, has no direct contact with reality. The basic reason for this is that reason knows universals, and, according to Ockham's Nominalism, everything real is individual. Nominalism reduces reality to individuals and reduces universals (essences, natures, species, kinds) to mere names (*nomina*). (This is a typically modern assumption, the reduction of "categories" to "man-made convenient groupings" rather than "real, natural kinds.")

Since it is reason that knows universals, the reduction of universals to names is a radical reduction of reason's power and value. It naturally tends to skepticism, though that was not Ockham's conclusion, but the conclusion drawn more and more by subsequent thinkers, until, after four centuries that did not produce a single great philosopher, Descartes confronted a culture in which the more intelligent one was, the more skeptical one tended to be, and constructed such a radically new reply to skepticism that he is called "the father of modern philosophy."

### "Ockham's Razor" and Nominalism

Hamlet said, to Horatio, "There are more things in heaven and earth, Horatio, than are dreamed of in your philosophy." For Ockham, there are *fewer* things in heaven and earth (i.e., reality) than in our common, traditional philosophy. The task of philosophy is to reduce, not to amplify. Thinking is primarily critical, destructive rather than constructive.

You might wonder, quite naturally, what is the appeal of such a negative and reductionistic philosophy. The answer is probably the love of simple explanations. "**A plurality of entities is not to be posited without necessity**"—this principle, now called "Ockham's Razor," was not invented by Ockham (in fact even Aristotle taught it, and Aquinas quotes it (in his second objection to God's existence: see page 85), for it is a common-sensical principle). But it was used more radically by Ockham than by anyone before him. What makes positing an entity "necessary" for Ockham is nothing but the law of non-contradiction. (David Hume would say something very similar four centuries later.)

One consequence of the Razor for Ockham is Empiricism: only empirical knowing (sense perception) touches objective reality as it really is.

Another is Nominalism: reality is simplified when universals are subtracted from it. This includes (1) Platonic Ideas, separate from concrete things, (2) Aristotelian-Thomistic forms, inherent in things, and also (3) Scotus's "common natures" which he had taught were indifferent to either universality, which they acquired in the mind, or individuality, which they acquired in reality by the "thisness" (*hecceitas*) that was the principle (source) of individuation.

If nothing real is universal, why do universal terms work? They seem to express universal concepts, which seem to express something universal in reality. Why can we classify all dogs in one species and all cats in another? As Chesterton argued, "If (as Nominalists claim) 'all chairs are different,' how can we call them all 'chairs'?"

Ockham answers: Since only individuals exist, all concepts are about individuals ("singulars") either distinctly known or confusedly known. Concepts that we *use* universally, to refer to more than one individual, are confused ways of referring to many individuals. Rather than use individual proper names for each dog or cat or chair, we invent vague terms like 'dog' and 'cat' or 'chair' out of convenience: it saves time. (A very simple explanation!)

Another concept Ockham criticizes as unnecessary is the concept of "species," which previous philosophers had used to mediate between a subjective universal concept and an objective universal form as the means by which we know the natures of real things.

Ockham also eliminates the distinction between active and passive intellect, since the role of the active intellect is to abstract universals, but universals are no longer there for Nominalism.

The resulting philosophical picture resembles that of Hume and modern early "analytic philosophy," in not accepting any truth claim unless it could be verified by sense observation or by the law of non-contradiction.

### Ockham's Theology and Causal Relationships

Even Ockham admits that reason can prove a first efficient cause, which faith calls "God," but he says we cannot know anything about it, since we have neither sense experience, nor a univocal concept, nor an analogical concept, of this being. We cannot prove that this cause is infinite, or perfect, or free, or even singular (reason cannot refute polytheism), or even that it is the first efficient cause of *all* things. All that depends on faith alone.

Since God is omnipotent (and this we know only by faith, not by reason), He can do anything that does not directly involve a logical self-contradiction (such as both existing and not existing at the same time and in the same sense). He can create an effect without a cause, e.g., the sight of a star without a star, or the memory of yesterday in our minds without there having been a yesterday. He "**can make the past not to have been.**" He can create in our minds an idea of something that in no way exists.

Therefore the traditional medieval program of *fides quaerens intellectum* ("faith seeking understanding") is a vain quest; we cannot throw any light on the mysteries of revealed theology by reason. E.g., we cannot solve the problem of evil (why does a wholly good God allow evil?) by arguing that even God cannot force man to do good all the time and yet preserve his free will because this is an intrinsic impossibility in the very essence of freedom. We cannot argue like this because for a Nominalist, we can deduce nothing from any essences because there are no essences. The Platonic tradition here comes to a dead end.

This skepticism extends also to anthropology. We cannot prove we have a soul or that it is spiritual and immortal.

Ockham deduces from his theology of omnipotence the same essential teaching about causality that David Hume was to deduce four centuries later from his epistemology of radical empiricism: that there is no real causal force or relation in reality, since we cannot sense it. ("Relation," in fact, is another universal that is only mental and not real, for Ockham; every real thing is quite separate and distinct from every other thing.) What we mistakenly think of as a real causal relation of one being (the cause) communicating something of its energy, motion, or even of its own nature to another being (e.g., a bat hitting a ball, or parents procreating children) is nothing but (that typical formula again!) a repeatedly observed sequence. Over and over again we see eggs come from birds, and it is not reality or reason but mere psychological habit that "causes" (!) us to think that birds *cause* ("lay") eggs. (This would be a very convenient philosophy for those accused of committing (causing) crimes.)

It also follows from Ockham's critique of causality, and from his Nominalism, that every real entity is independent of every other one. There is no real causal dependence. Anything can exist with or without anything else. Everything in the universe sings, "I did it my way."

## Ockham's Ethics

One's ethics always depends on one's metaphysics. Medieval philosophers before Ockham had viewed goodness as a universal property of being. Thus morality links man to God, the supreme good. By being good, man participates in God's goodness. Ockham severs this bond. "Participation" is another category that simply drops out of the Nominalist's vocabulary. Everything real is individual and separate, including God and man.

Morality, then, depends not on goodness, either divine goodness or natural human goodness, not on the divine nature or on human nature, or on man's natural end or purpose or final cause, all of which are universals, and therefore only names. Morality depends only on God's will and man's moral obligation to obey it.

God willed commandments. He could have willed others. It is the will alone that determines oughtness, or obligation. Moral goodness is nothing but (that typical formula for Ockham) the conformity of an inferior will to a superior will. Therefore we can speak of human goodness, in this limited way, but we cannot speak of divine goodness, since there is no will superior to God's that would allow us to speak of God's conformity to that will. So we cannot even meaningfully say that "God is good."

So we must obey God not because He is good but because He is all-powerful. Power trumps goodness; "might makes right" for God. (If one believes this, one is naturally tempted to draw the conclusion that "might makes right" for man too, though Ockham's Christian faith forced him to deny this conclusion.)

This is Euthyphro versus Socrates, and it is the philosophy of the Muslim Ash'arites. An act is good only because God wills it, not because it is reasonable, or perfects human nature, or helps man to attain his end, whether that end is Heaven, happiness, saintliness, or all three.

Scotus had reduced the scope of the (universal) natural moral law to the first three Commandments; Ockham eliminated it altogether. God could have commanded anything, and that sheer fact would have made it morally good, or right, to do. He could even have commanded us to hate Him or our neighbor, and then we would be morally obliged to hate Him, and loving Him or our neighbor would be sinful. God is completely arbitrary and irrational. Ockham demeans reason not only for man but even for God.

The historical proof that Ockham's "modern way" was a disaster, not just for medieval philosophy but for philosophy itself, is the fact that there was not a single great systematic philosopher of lasting influence for the next 400 years, until Descartes. Scholastic philosophy turned to extremely abstract arguments about words between competing schools, so that "the philosopher" became a comical theatrical stereotype, especially in French drama. The closest thing to great philosophical thinkers are poetic mystics: Nicholas of Cusa, Meister Eckhart, Paracelsus, Boehme, Bruno, and St. John of the Cross (who was philosophically a Thomist, not an Ockhamist). Between Ockham and Descartes, there were great minds, but they were all in the sciences or the arts. The great medieval issue of the relation between religion (the eternal thing) and philosophy (the old thing) had been replaced by the problem of the relation between religion and the new thing, modern science. Philosophy re-entered the "great conversation" only when Descartes joined science and philosophy in his experiment of doing philosophy itself by the scientific method. Philosophy, having divorced its first wife, religion, would marry and serve a second, modern science.

# 53. Meister Eckhart (1260–1328)

Meister ("Master") Eckhart was a German mystical philosopher, though perhaps not himself a mystic. Even though some of his apparently pantheistic theses were labeled heretical by the Church, he was very influential, and he always thought of himself as orthodox.

His apparent pantheism came from teaching that **there is nothing outside of** (or in addition to) **God**. Creatures exist, but only "within" God.

Eckhart uses two different language systems to make this point. On the one hand, when he comments on scripture, Eckhart uses ordinary, traditional language and identifies God with being; but then he makes the non-traditional point that nothing else has being in itself. Creatures are called beings not because they have any being in themselves but only because they are *related to* God, who alone is being. They exist only with God's existence, not with their own.

This is, of course, pantheism if taken literally, i.e., if he means exactly what he says: that existence is identical to God and that creatures have no act of existence of their own but exist only with God's act of existence. This goes much farther than the traditional, orthodox point that creatures are totally *contingent,* i.e., *dependent* on God for their existence. It says that in themselves, creatures are simply nothing. It seems to deny that God created them.

He answers the charge of pantheism by saying that **God is in the world as the soul is in the body.** This analogy does fit God's *omnipresence* (the soul is totally present to every part of the body), *causality* (the soul causes the body's life), and *existential dependence.* The body does not exist as a human body when the soul no longer exists in it; it does not have its own act of existence; if it did, it would be a second substance. And Eckhart's analogy allows creatures to have their own identity, not God's since the body has its own identity: it is not the soul.

On the other hand, in his more philosophical passages, he uses a different terminology and denies that God has being, on the Neoplatonic ground that being is inherently creaturely and that Intellect, or mind, is superior to being. Here he is using Neoplatonic philosophical terminology rather than ordinary language. (There is a natural connection between Neoplatonic metaphysics and esoterism (look it up!).)

This Neoplatonic philosophical terminology is similar to that of Pseudo-Dionysius the Areopagite and Scotus Erigena: calling God "super-being" or "hyper-being" or even "non-being" or "nothing" because of (a) an unusually "low" notion of "being" as something inherently creaturely, and (b) an unusually "high" notion of "Intellect" as inherently Godlike and absolute, not relative to being. In modern philosophy this will be called Idealism: making being relative to mind rather than mind relative to being.

Eckhart argues for the thesis that intellect is superior to being as follows:

(a) It is more perfect to exist and to understand than simply to exist.

(b) Although God seems to have revealed His name as Being ("I am Who am," Ex. 3:14), this was not a revealing but a concealing, a hiding, according to Eckhart.

(c) St. John did not say, "In the beginning was being" but "In the beginning was the Logos." Christ also said "I am the Truth" (Jn 14:6).

God, however, for Eckhart is even superior to Intellect, Mind, or Logos as well as to being. Thus Eckhart's images of God as "a darkness," "a wilderness," and "a desert." The best term for God is Plotinus's "One" or "unity." As in Plotinus, Intellect is superior to being(s), and The One is superior to Intellect.

This One is, for Eckhart, more absolute than the plurality of Persons in the Trinity. The unitary divine nature transcends the plurality of Persons. In orthodox Trinitarian theology, the one divine nature and the three divine Persons are equally primordial and absolute. But for Eckhart "the Godhead" is the transcendent "source" of the three Trinitarian Persons.

Here are some of Eckhart's more striking apparently heretical sayings:

(1) **There is something in the soul that is uncreated and uncreatable. If the whole soul were of such a nature, it would be uncreated and uncreatable. And this is the intellect.** (I.e., the intellect is not a creature but inherently divine and uncreated.)

(2) (In mystical experience**) we are transformed totally into God and are converted into Him in a similar manner as in the Sacrament the bread is converted into the Body of Christ. I am converted into Him in such a way that He makes me one being with Himself, not a similar being . . . there is no distinction.**

(3) **Whatever the holy scriptures say of Christ is wholly true of every good and divine man . . . whatever is proper to the divine nature is entirely proper to the just and divine man . . . such a man brings about whatever God brings about, and he created heaven and earth together with God. He is the begetter of the eternal Word, and without such a man God would not be able to do anything.**

Eckhart's defense of such statements is that they are meant esoterically and not literally, and that he intended his doctrine to be nothing contradictory to the orthodox teaching of the Church. Yet 28 of his sayings were officially condemned in 1329. If creeds mean anything at all, lines have to be drawn in the sand somewhere, as a matter of logical definition.

# 54. Nicholas of Cusa (1401–1464)

Nicholas Kryfts (no known relation to the author) was born in Cues (Latin, Cusa) on the Moselle river opposite Bernkastel, source of famous Bernkasteler wines. Over 300 of his manuscripts are still preserved there, with his handwritten marginal comments. (In one of his little dialogs, an uneducated Roman street worker teaches a philosopher how to pitch a curve in a ball game.)

He is the greatest philosopher between Ockham and Descartes. Like most philosophers, he was a prodigy, and the kind of universal genius that could exist only in premodern times (Leibnitz was probably the last one), mastering all the scientific, literary, philosophical, and theological knowledge of his time, as well as Latin, Greek, and Hebrew.

He was educated by the Brothers of the Common Life (as were Thomas à Kempis and Erasmus, later). He entered the University of Padua at 16 and was sent in 1437 as the Pope's legate to Greece and Constantinople to prepare for the reunion of the Eastern and Western branches of the Church. The reunion succeeded, for a short time, at the Council of Florence in 1438. He was made a cardinal in 1445, even though he admired the writings of Eckhart, which were questionable in their orthodoxy. In his philosophical theory as well as in his political practice he was a unifier, a synthesizer, a harmonizer of opposites.

Nicholas believed that this reconciliation was made difficult more for philosophical reasons than theological ones, specifically because of the reliance on Aristotelian logic. He preferred the mystical unity of Plotinus to the logical distinctions of Aristotle, since the latter defines the differences between factions and their ideas, but the former realizes deeper, hidden ways in which they are one.

## Infinity

However, Nicholas was a Christian theologian, not a Plotinian philosopher. His distinctive notion, that of the divine infinity, is a distinctively Christian one.

Duns Scotus had already centered his theology on it, as God's most distinctive attribute. He had distinguished between the lesser notion of infinity, which even Aristotle admitted (namely, infinity in causal power through time: a causal chain need not ever end), and the greater one, which was infinity in being. The latter was possessed only by the God of the Bible. It, and its correlative notion of creation out of nothing, had never entered into a pagan mind. (The Hebrew word, *bara'*, has no equivalent in any other ancient language, and is predicated of God alone.)

## Socratic Ignorance

In the fifteenth century nearly every one of many rival philosophical sects claimed to be teaching the philosophy of Aristotle. Nicholas concluded that their common error was an ignorance of Socrates and his "lesson one," the knowledge of their own ignorance. He titled one of his most famous treatises *On Learned Ignorance.* Its main point is that the wiser one is, the more he knows how much he does not know. This, says Nicholas, was true not only of Socrates but also of Aristotle, who compared our attempts to understand the highest beings to owls blinking at the sun. It is not just a matter of "critical thinking," or a skeptical attitude. It is a matter of metaphysics.

And this inadequacy of human reason is especially crucial when its object is the Christian God, or infinity. The finite and the infinite are "incommensurable" (not related even by proper analogy); there is no proportion between them. Precision, or clarity, or exactness, is simply impossible here. All distinctions between finite concepts vanish in the light of mystical vision.

Although Aquinas said almost the same thing, Nicholas opposes his "learned ignorance" to what he called "ignorant learnedness" for which he blames the Aristotelians and Thomists, who make the mistake of trying to deal with the infinite by means of the finite instead of dealing with the finite in terms of the infinite and therefore being satisfied with inadequacy, approximation, and paradox. (A paradox is an apparent, but not ultimately real, contradiction.)

## Reason vs. Intuition

Reason fails to lead us to the infinite, Nicholas says. He compares our rational knowledge of truth to a polygon inscribed in a circle: an infinite number of sides can be added to such a polygon but it will never be identical with the circle. The difference is not quantitative, but one of dimension. Compare the point of Plato's "Cave": not just new ideas but a new *kind* of "Idea," a new metaphysical category, a new kind of reality, a new "world" (*kosmos*, order).

Reason is discursive: it moves from subject to predicate and from premise to conclusion, comparing and relating different definable concepts that are finite and relative to each other. It cannot deal with the non-finite, the non-definable, the non-relative, the non-different, and the non-conceptual.

Reason's ultimate principle is the principle of non-contradiction. This does not allow us to grasp the unity of diverse perfections in God (e.g., justice and mercy, universality and individuality, oneness and manyness). For that, a higher power is needed, which Nicholas calls Intellect. This is a power of insight or intuition, and it sees the unity in, above, or under the distinctions seen by reason.

Thus Nicholas blames Aristotle's logic for impeding the mind's progress to the true God. This logic cannot admit **the coincidence (identity) of opposites,** which is the essential principle of mystical theology, and which appears at infinity. This is why Nicholas ranks Neoplatonism above Aristotelianism.

## The Coincidence of Opposites in God

Nicholas wants to call God the greatest, or "the maximum." Book I of *On Learned Ignorance* is about the absolute maximum, which is God; Book II is about the relative maximum, or the created universe; and Book III is about the coincidence of these two opposites in the incarnate Christ.

Like Anselm, Nicholas calls God "that being than which nothing greater can exist." The absolute maximum (God) means the being infinitely rich in perfection, so that nothing can be added to it, restrict it, or stand in opposition to it. It is both the absolute fullness of being and absolute unity, since unity is really identical with being. (Actually, all these theses can be found also in Aquinas.) The fact that Nicholas calls God both "infinite" and "being" shows that he is not a Neoplatonist, for the Neoplatonists considered infinity a negative idea and being a necessarily finite and inferior one.

Much later, Hegel was to construct an entire thought system on the radically new logical structure of contradiction rather than non-contradiction, on a somewhat similar (but also different) "coincidence of opposites," in his famous "dialectic" of thesis versus antithesis unified in a synthesis.

## The Mathematics of Infinity

Nicholas called mathematics "**the science of the infinite**," and used many mathematical symbols for his "coincidence of opposites," especially the identity of the infinite minimum and the infinite maximum. He says, for instance, that a line with maximum straightness will also be the maximum in circularity; for an infinitely or absolutely straight line means a line of minimum curvature. Now as you increase the size of any circle, the curvature of the circumference decreases, so that the circumference of the greatest possible circle will have the smallest possible curvature and be absolutely straight. So an infinite circle is identical with a straight line. And a circle of infinite radius is also a straight line. Nicholas also says that the infinity of points on a straight line, however large, can be represented by the points of a finite segment of it, however small; and this shows that infinity is present in "contracted" form in every finite thing.

Thus geometry is a natural analogy of metaphysics. In fact, says Nicholas, it is the best way. The only other way is from ordinary language, which is the way of Socrates, Plato, and Aristotle.

The mathematical way goes back to Parmenides and Pythagoras and to the famous formula of Hermes Trismegistus, the semi-mythical ancient Egyptian mystic, that God is "an infinite sphere whose circumference is nowhere and whose center is everywhere."

In Pascal and other modern mathematicians this becomes a formula for *nature,* and implies the proto-Einsteinian idea that there is no absolute space, no absolute center, no absolute standard of reference in the universe. Thus the earth is displaced as the absolute center of the universe by these philosophers even before it was displaced scientifically by Copernicus. As Pascal says, *"Nothing stands still for us."* The only absolute rest would be infinite velocity, where we find the "coincidence of opposites." (Thus God is everywhere, and needs to go nowhere, and thus is at complete rest because He moves with infinite speed.)

Many other Christian theologians, including St. Anselm and St. Bonaventure, had also used mathematical analogies for God's infinity. Some had even compared the Trinity to a triangle with three right angles, because at infinity, all figures become one, for as Nicholas says, **infinity is where all possibles are actualized.** (Would Aquinas agree with this? Why or why not?)

## Theological Implications

Nicholas's assertion that God is both totally transcendent to all creatures and totally immanent (present) to them is not unique, but traditional; but what he deduces from it is new: Since God is in everything in a non-finite way, it follows that **everything is in everything else.** Nicholas quotes this saying of Anaxagoras and gives it a new meaning. He uses the illustration of a single face reflected in many mirrors; each mirror reflects not only the one face but also every other image of it. He calls this **contraction**: every finite thing contracts the whole universe in it, the microcosm mirroring the macrocosm. He also makes a serious joke on Anaxagoras's formula, saying that **everything is in everything—and inversely.**

This is the basic unity, or co-presence, of all things. It is not pantheism, because creatures are not annihilated and God remains infinitely transcendent. But it is as far from deism (the "absent God" of Aristotle) as possible.

There is actually a close theological parallel in Aquinas: since God is the infinite act of existence, He both (1) transcends all finite essences *and* (2) is most intimately present in them, as that which makes them actual rather than merely potential—by the exact same reason: His infinity. (See page 89–90.) Aquinas, however, does not conceive infinity mathematically or quantitatively. And he does not draw the conclusion that creatures, like God, are also universally present to each other.

In this typically medieval cosmology man occupies the unique place of being simultaneously spiritual and material, angelic and animal, thus linking and unifying two worlds. This is one of the ways he is the image of God, uniting in himself opposite perfections. He is the whole of reality in miniature, the microcosm ("little cosmos") reflecting and being reflected by the macrocosm ("big cosmos"). He is mineral, vegetable, animal, and spirit at once and as one.

## The New Cosmology

This departs radically from the traditional Aristotelian cosmology. For Aristotle, the universe is a finite sphere with the earth at its motionless center and surrounded by median spheres of moon, sun, planets, and fixed stars. There is thus an absolute center, an absolute rest, and an absolute direction, up and down. For Nicholas none of this holds true anymore. The universe images God by having no circumference. It also images nothingness by having no center. Everything moves, including the earth. In fact, both motion and place, for Nicholas, are relative to the observer: a remarkable presaging of relativity theory.

Our reason seeks finitude, absolute reference points, and non-contradiction. The universe, imaging God as it does, refuses to provide us with these things. Therefore our reason is radically inadequate to understand not only the Creator but even the creature. Aristotle's logic of finitude is not only inadequate for conceiving the absolutely-infinite God but also the relatively-infinite cosmos. It is also inadequate for Christianity, for its achievement is to distinguish, while a logic of the Christian God should unite.

This "mismatch" between finite reason and infinite reality is the ultimate reason for the necessity of "learned ignorance": it is the only possible match between our mind and reality. Of even the cosmos Nicholas would say what Aquinas says of God: that the very summit of knowledge of it is the knowledge that we do not have this knowledge.

## Influence

Though a "fringe" philosopher, Nicholas's ideas percolated pregnantly (to use a badly mixed metaphor) among subsequent philosophers, theologians, and scientists. The standard view of medieval philosophy is that it was uninterested in natural science and held back scientific progress by idolizing the authority of Aristotle. The first is almost universally false. The medievals were fascinated with the cosmos, but were groping their way slowly to the modern scientific method for revealing it. The second charge is certainly not true of thinkers like Nicholas of Cusa, who was liberating the mind from its confines and opening up a door to an open and infinite cosmos.